DIFFERENT & DEFICIENT

*How Education Can Make
People Believe That Different is Bad*

BY: DR. ARMSTEAD

© Copyright 2022 by Dr. Armstead

All rights reserved. The contents of this book may not be reproduced, duplicated, or transmitted without direct written permission from the author.

Under no circumstances will any legal responsibility or blame be held against the publisher for any reparation, damages, or monetary loss due to the information herein, either directly or indirectly.

TABLE OF CONTENTS

Introduction 1

Chapter 1
   Money 3

Chapter 2
   Time 25

Chapter 3
   Dress Codes 40

Chapter 4
   Educational Trauma 57

Chapter 5
   Trust 64

Chapter 6
   Students 78

Chapter 7
   Administration 96

Chapter 8
   Teamwork 106

Chapter 9
   Future Teachers 120

Chapter 10
   Dismissal 131

INTRODUCTION

If you think this book is going to be a cute text about amazing teaching stories...you're wrong. If you think this is going to help you remember all the educational code words and terminology...you're wrong. In fact, this book may actually convince you that you're in the wrong field and need to leave. This book ultimately may show you that to teach is to be called, and a calling to teach comes with pain at times!

What this book won't do however, is convince you to quit your job and blame it on the author and their personal experiences. Instead the goal is transparency! The hope is that by the end of this book, the life experiences, the pains, and the joys will inspire you to be a better teacher, or a better mentor to youth outside of the field of education. It is not completely true that everyone in the field of education should be there. In fact, some individuals currently in the field of education are there because of who they know, rather than what they can do! I'm sure just by reading this paragraph there are a few teachers, whether past or present, that popped into your mind. Now don't get me wrong, I have tons to be grateful for as a teacher with many years under my belt. I also know some amazing teachers past and present. But c'mon, you know there are a handful of teachers you looked at and said "Why in the heck did anyone hire you?"

That is why I wrote this book! I am one of very few teachers that actually do enjoy teaching, but sadly am being pushed out. We could all say it's because of the low pay, large class sizes, or even the disrespect of students and parents. However, at the end of the day it's a continual revolving door of teachers, because of the culture of the field and individual schools. Some individuals would believe that teachers are the toughest people in the world, because of all that we had to endure during the last few school years. However, what others see as tough skin is actually what is known as self-sacrifice...an unhealthy norm for many teachers.

After many years of teaching, three degree programs (Bachelors, Masters, Doctorate), and teaching in two totally different regions of the U. S., I have become washed out. I have worked both in general education and alternative education, elementary and middle school, collegiate, full-time and part-time, and it still stands that my heart became broken when the culture of education became so toxic and negative.

Now that I have your attention, you clearly see it is easy to complain in this field. However, that's the point of this book...Take the negative and use it to become a better teacher, or take it and use it as the platform for your skills and heart with youth elsewhere, where it is more beneficial!

CHAPTER 1

Money

When I first became interested in teaching I was only in middle school. I can't remember the exact date or time like some can, but I remember the exact moment it happened. This same feeling returned in high school during AP Psychology, but by that time I was already on a mission. The feeling that I'm speaking about is frustration mixed with a little anger. Now that I think about it, most of my greatest aspirations come from frustration.

Anyway, I can remember sitting in my 7th grade math class feeling very frustrated and vengeful from what had happened the previous day. The day before, I was sitting at the same desk, with the same teacher, with a puddle of tears the size of a lake on my desk. We were learning about a concept of math that clearly confused me. I don't know if it was the band class prior to and how much I was being bullied, or simply that my pre-teen brain at the time was having a mood swing of its own. All I can remember all this time later was that I felt dumb, I felt ignorant, I felt hopeless, and all because I simply asked a question more than once. I specifically remember seeing everyone around me look back and laugh as the teacher projected across the room, "Maybe if you were paying attention and not talking you would understand what I was telling you!". Those snickers, giggles, and the grim smile on my teacher's face still haunt me to this day.

I never told my parents about this experience until I was a teacher myself for various reasons. First of all, how embarrassing would it have been to have your parents come into the school and curse your teacher out! I mean, don't get me wrong, I'm not saying cursing out a teacher is EVER right, but no student should ever neglect parental support. I mean in this society right now if a parent wants to get involved, no matter how wrong and out of pocket it may seem to us as teachers, it's a time of celebration that they are even supporting and engaged. That's a topic for another day, but if you're an engaged and involved parent, take this as me extending my arms to you for a hug, because I appreciate you!

The other reason I never told my parents was because the child-like behavior of my teacher at the time gave me a huge sense of motivation! At times, even when I was young, the things that would infuriate others and knock them off track actually made me want to work harder. This could actually be the reason why after many trials and tribulations in this field, I have actually become a much better teacher than I was at the start in 2006/2007. In fact, I won't even say that it could be the reason, because I know that it is indeed the reason why I teach the way that I do. Some would say that I have a huge heart for students and youth overall, but little do they know it is because most of the time I can see myself in them, and want to make sure they don't make the mistakes that I did early on.

Anyhow, after all this time and years that have gone by, I can envision this classroom, this loud response of my teacher, the lie he sold to the principal that got me in trouble, and how much I wanted to flip the desk like Hulk but instead held it in. THAT was the start of my goal to become a teacher to make things better. My mission was to become a teacher in the field so that I could show others what a teacher really is, what you're supposed to utilize as your foundation for why you do everything you do, and of course to make sure that no future student would EVER feel the way that I felt by another adult in the classroom.

This is probably the weirdest reason you have ever heard from an adult who went into the field of education. I understand that, and I actually laugh when others say that, because to me this is why more should go into the field of education. I didn't line up my dolls as a little girl, I didn't make my cousins suffer through a fake lesson plan I did as a child, and I didn't even like most of my teachers growing up. As a result of that, it was like someone supplying me with power from a plug, so that I could be a phenomenal future teacher who would correct all of these scars from my educational journey!

What I have come to find out and realize by doing this, is that the real currency, the real money in engaging students is not made with paper. If you piled the classroom from floor to ceiling with stacks of money and coins, it

STILL would not change a thing. Well, I mean, you would have excitement all around, students makin' it rain, and some teachers contemplating early retirement, but a better learning environment? As my middle school students always say when they don't like something...THAT'S CAP!

I know money does in fact help schools in ways that I could never reach the end of, but it is not the sole solution to a better educational experience for individual students. Money won't solve trauma. Money won't solve suicidal ideations. Money won't solve teacher burn-out leading to lack of motivation in the classroom. Money won't solve teacher shortages. Money won't solve student defiance. Money won't solve low parental engagement or involvement. Money won't solve missed learning post-quarantine. Money won't solve PTSD from students experiencing loss. Money won't solve childhood emotional neglect. Money won't solve large class sizes. Money won't solve EVERY problem we currently see in education, because if it did I wouldn't have a need to write this book!

Money does in fact solve a lot of the curricular and resourceful deficiencies we see, but what money in education can't do is:

Make
Opportunities
New
Every day for
Youth

In education we have to get back to the foundation of what we exist for. We are in existence to exchange something from the adult mind to youth that is of value. This valuable "medium of exchange" (the thing we are transferring from adults to youth) isn't something that is only beneficial to one party and not the other. Instead it should be mutually beneficial. It should be something that is noticeably absent, something difficult to survive without, something that cannot be individually produced. This "medium of exchange" should most importantly be defined clearly by both parties. To define it, adults must first recognize that they aren't in control of the future, but in fact our students are and that's why the true money making solution...the product that **M**akes **O**pportunities **N**ew **E**very day for **Y**outh is CONNECTING CULTURES!

Let me flip this a little bit...Every day, Every Hour, Every Moment in every classroom should be centered on money (Making Opportunities New Every day for Youth). Of course I'm not talking about dollar bills, I'm talking about what should always be happening in classrooms across the nation every day! Making Opportunities New Every day for Youth!! This means every day making a new connection, a new relationship, or a new method of teaching the same content, so that students never disengage or detach the way I did starting in 7th grade. This isn't simple, and it may have been said before, but I bet not from the experiences that I have had in these last 15 years and will share throughout this book.

Students disengage because within education there is no making, no new, and sadly in some situations no youth!

As we come out of quarantine life (because the pandemic still brews), we have become so consumed with adult concerns, adult feelings, what adults think is best, and we have essentially forgotten that the success of our legacy in the field as teachers is determined by how successful youth are! Doesn't seem truthful right? Seems like it should be related to something else or someone else? Well, then let's go back to my experience that started this chapter...

I was in tears in my 7th grade math class, and left enough of them to fill Lake Michigan. Why? Because I had asked a question of my teacher, and in his frustration he didn't want to explain again. Maybe it was inconvenient, time wasting, irritating, or most of all, maybe it was a trigger of some sort for whatever reason that day. No matter what the reason was, that is his legacy with me! This is not only what I will always remember about my 7th grade math teacher, but also what my memories will always remind me of when it comes to math. No matter the progression I made overall as an adult who has accomplished various things in math, I will reflect back to math not being my favorite subject because of this experience. This is the legacy left within my soul when math is mentioned or presented to me! This is also the legacy created and left behind for that 7th grade math teacher. Other students may have had better experiences than I did with him, but the legacy he leaves behind (what was handed down to me from this adult) is the fact that his personal life or career life created an adverse reaction towards me.

In other words, this was the experience that would forever stain my views of math, allow my math skills to model the image of swiss cheese, taint my feelings towards anything that involved abstract thinking for many years, and created further academic setbacks in my K-12th grade career because these skills were lost. Am I blaming this teacher? NO! Instead, what I'm doing is painting a picture for you. This picture is a literal example of what happens when connecting cultures aka M.O.N.E.Y. (Making Opportunities New Every day for Youth) is not included in the classroom. You end up with disconnection, disengagement, and long-term deficiencies. Deficiencies that create anger, frustration, self-harm, high suspension rates, etc. What these experiences do is create cracks that later become sink holes because they were not addressed early on.

The reason I seem to be "stuck" on this experience is because it was math, and I'm sure there are thousands of students who can relate to this. It isn't just math that they don't like, it's the lack of connection they had while in math class, and the experiences that constantly replay in their minds when in math class or any other subject that they do not feel completely competent in. These experiences constantly remind the student, or sometimes even adults, that although they may be successful in a math concept right now…"Don't forget that you're trash in other areas, you're still insufficient!". It may not even be just math or English, it is any subject in any class where the teacher either reacted the same way that my teacher did, or did not take the intentional time to connect with the cultures of students in the classroom, so that education was individualized and not standardized.

DIFFERENT and DEFICIENT

I have talked to countless amounts of people who can recall experiences such as this from decades ago in classrooms across this nation. They are still, in a sense, dealing with the trauma or the abuse that it caused within their overall educational experience. This is not to say that every day there are some mean and crazy teachers out to abuse, confuse, and lose students academically, but instead there are children daily in school that are experiencing things that we don't realize as adults, are leaving a lasting legacy. Instead of covering our own experiences up and avoiding the conversation with our students, we should instead be more open and transparent, so that they can see we are in fact just older versions of them! Doing this would then allow for a more humanistic education, and more teachers connecting with the hearts and souls of students rather than just their brain and triggered emotions.

Insufficiency and adverse educational experiences were things that plagued me for years, no matter the experience, or what level of education I obtained. Insufficiency in math and insufficiency in my ability to make M.O.N.E.Y. in the classroom crippled me for many years. I can remember even now the days I would sit on the bed in my room with my laptop and aimlessly search for jobs I could do that no longer required me to remain in the field of education. It sounds bad, and I know some may take it the wrong way, but a teacher who hasn't had this debate at least once in their career is either suppressing it deeply, or on the brink of experiencing it soon. It is bound to happen, because we are trained to portray perfection rather than humanity, humility, and transparency in classrooms with students. We are trained that we are the adults, we are the masters of the content, we are the experts in the field, and that means that any signs of weakness equates to us being "trash".

In my own experience I couldn't have been more human and transparent with my students than in the 2020-2021 school year! In this school year, not only was I teaching online the entire time (something I had previous experience with from being an online full-time faculty member at a university), but I was also teaching ALL academic subject areas with 7th grade...including MATH!!!! You can imagine how anxious I was about teaching math, but I was also anxious about how I was going to make M.O.N.E.Y. (connections) with students exclusively through a laptop. I guess you could say in some sense, even before I wrote this chapter, I was putting this M.O.N.E.Y. concept into practice.

When I was working with these students online, there were many times that I would have to correct myself, they would correct me, or I would just humbly admit I didn't know the answer (things I NEVER saw my teachers or other teachers doing). Of course when I didn't know the answer, the class and I would go through and find the answer in a way that not only I understood, but the students who felt the same confusion would understand as well. Despite what most would assume, my students did not think less of my skills as a teacher, and neither did they become more disrespectful...I don't know where that train of thought in education even comes from. In fact, most of my students in that school year shared how they felt more competent knowing that their teacher makes mistakes just the same as they do! I can remember one student saying "I've never had a teacher admit to not being good at a subject." Another student said "I like how you don't get mad when we don't know, but instead you break it down to us again and again until we get it!" One of my favorite things that a student said that year was "I used to hate math, but now that I get it I almost love it!" This my dear valued and appreciated reader is M.O.N.E.Y made in the classroom! This is what it means to connect with the culture of students in your classroom, and make sure that they feel seen, heard, and appreciated just the same way you would want them to be with you.

Remember M.O.N.E.Y. made or had in the classroom is not dollar bills and coins. It's not checks and grants limited to where it can be spent. M.O.N.E.Y. in classrooms, at least the REAL M.O.N.E.Y. is connecting cultures! Connecting the cultures of yourself and your students in the classroom takes time, takes humility, takes intentionality, takes trust, and most of all takes breaking out of the norm and ways of doing things that have always been done! Connecting cultures in the classroom means discomfort in adults at times, so that your legacy is youthminded and not you-minded. This also makes sure that your legacy is loving and motivational beyond the school site.

Wait, hold on, let me step back and bring some clarity to what I'm really talking about when I say culture in this conversation, before someone assumes its only ethnicity or whatever other controversial terms are flying around in society right now. By culture, let me start first by telling you what I am NOT talking about! When I say culture I am NOT talking about race! When I say culture I am NOT talking about sexual preference! When I say culture I am NOT talking about religious point of views. When I say culture I am NOT talking about politics or anything related to the political realm right now (I have never aspired to get into politics). When I say culture I AM talking about family structure, holiday traditions, musical preferences, food preferences, hobbies, clothes, appropriate body language, etc. If you notice culture is WHO we are and not WHAT we are. This is why I say it is an intentional action of teachers to learn the culture of their students, because you have to speak TO and WITH them non-academically to find out WHO they are!

I know, some of you may be saying " who and what you are is the same thing." Yes, I can understand that in some sense, but at the same time I also see it differently (I told you I see things differently than the average teacher). Who you are is what you think about yourself and what you know about yourself fully from the heart. What you are is what others say about you and how they label you. Who I am is what people do not see, it's what I feel in my emotions and listen to in my thoughts. Who I am is also what most people don't know about me, because no one knows the soul of the person except the person itself, and neither can others be completely accurate in stating your intentions without being in your skin. To know who I am fully, you have to take time out to talk with me without judgment. Who I am, by my internal definition, is a passionate adult for the advocacy of youth. Who I am, is an empath that can't stand to hurt or offend others. Who I am is dedicated to education and dedicated to improving my thought life.

What you are is most often confused with who you are, because when people say things about you or label you it then gets into your thoughts and emotions. What you are, is typically stated by other people and groups, because like I mentioned before, they are not in your skin to know the 100% truth about you. What you are is judgments, biases, assumptions, and usually what others use as a way to label you comfortably, so that they are less intimidated or uncomfortable around you. What I am is a black woman. What I am is a single mother (by way of divorce). What I am is 38 years old. What I am is a teacher. What I am is a woman with an afro. What I am is what others can see, but who I am is the soul deep truths that I feel, know, and often don't communicate to explain why I say and do different things in and out of the classroom. What I am is able to be expressed in words when I pass on and transition to heaven.

Who I am will rise to heaven without words to bring them to fruition.

How many times do you see or hear of teachers really taking time during lesson planning to think of how the family structure of most of the students in the class will change how they teach a social studies or language arts concept? How many times have you heard or seen a teacher take into consideration the different styles of music that students listen to, so that the jingle they create to teach a math concept is enjoyed by all students? How many times have you heard or seen a teacher stop class and discuss a t-shirt or hoodie a student chose to wear, and why they like it or what it represents to them? How many times have you seen or heard of teachers in the classroom starting class with a mental health check-in, followed by a discussion on their own personal mental health? Probably pretty rare! Why? Because we have become an entity and field that is concerned more with the WHAT of a child rather than the WHO. Trends state that it takes too much time, and it's wasted time talking to students about who they are deeply on the inside.

We are trained that we must spend more time on the WHAT, so they can pass a test, standard, or assignment to the nation's satisfaction.

Sadly, this is why so many students have shown in many ways that they do not like school. It does not satisfy them, it does not make sense, it does not feel safe. Students daily spend more hours in classrooms with "random adults" than they do with their families, but these same adults don't know WHO these students really are. Time spent in the classroom with teachers is focused on uncomfortable experiences, mandated emulation, little consideration of emotional and social differences, all to make sure that a grade that may not even matter in the future career the student chooses is proficient.

There are times I have been in other classrooms observing, and when a student gets louder it is immediately equated to aggression or anger. Although the student was just passionate about the topic, wanted to really engage in the conversation, and was displaying to the teacher a part of how their family expresses passion (culture) in a conversation at home, the response was anger and a dismissal from the conversation or classroom. I have seen students who were dealing with grief at very young ages get into trouble because their peers said or did something that triggered their pain, and their reaction was to fight or use angry words towards them. When relaying this information to the administration (who didn't know why the child was newly overly aggressive), the response was "Well, everyone has to deal with death…they just need to get over it. They can't use that as an excuse for the rest of their life!" Keep in mind this was a 3rd grade student I gathered this information at the time.

THIS is what I mean when I say that M.O.N.E.Y. is not being made in the classroom! THIS is what I mean when I say that connecting cultures is important! THIS is what I mean when I say we need to pay more attention to bringing out the WHO in students instead of the WHAT in our students! All of this is important, because this is when you build on a currency that cannot be stolen or destroyed. It will also be the one thing that helps your students to be lifelong learners....their education is relatable and applicable, because it is about THEM! Their education is not filled with only academia, but instead it is also personal, authentic, and unique. This type of educational experience will help them to understand who they are at a young age, and push them to discover their purpose, rather than where they should gather a paycheck. This is something I only have seen a little less than a few handful of times in all of my 30+ years of pursuing education.

If professionals in education were all honest about ourselves and the education system, we would say that we really are not working within a system that fully supports the diverse beings of our students. The education system in the U.S. needs some major differentiation, because what is currently being done is not evolving and developing better citizens in society! What the current U.S. education system is continuing to do, is develop young adults into individuals that know who they are and what they want to leave behind on this earth when they are no longer here, but also feel that "who" they are is not as important as "what" they are according to others in becoming "successful". Who they are is being covered up or hidden behind masks (not literally) to satisfy the expectations of others in fulfilling a role, position, or goal for "societal success". Students are being taught to leave behind their inner feelings and desires, because it is less important than fitting a mold of "appropriate" to graduate, to get a job, or even to gain respect of the teacher at the front of the classroom. We are in a sense telling students to hide themselves, because right now the only important thing we need to do is "catch you up" and get you ready for the standardized test(s) at the end of the school year to show that I am in fact teaching and doing a good job every day.

I can remember teaching a young girl one year who initially came into my classroom very guarded and quiet. Even though she was amazing to me, and could teach me something new every day, she would not often talk to her peers, or even want to work in groups if there was a group project to be done. There was one day I remember most when she was discouraged by getting the incorrect answer, and almost immediately removed herself from the classroom (virtually). While at the time I couldn't stop class and go make sure she was ok, I did have it at the back of my mind to see if she was any different when she showed up in the next subject. Unfortunately, she did not show up again until the next day of class, and was sure to keep her camera off the entire time.

Before the day was over, I took the time to ask her to stay when everyone else was gone, so that I could chat with her for a little bit. Side note, try to get in the habit of saying that you want to chat with your students instead of saying you need to talk to them. Just like our boss, spouse, or any other authority figure can cause us to shake in fear when they say "we need to talk", that is the same way that students feel when we say the same thing. Anyway, I ended up talking with her for about 15 minutes after classes were over, and came to the knowledge that the very abrupt exit from class was because she felt embarrassed and didn't want to be in the class anymore. She thought that maybe everyone else was laughing or feeling a certain way about her because she didn't answer correctly. As you can imagine, the whole conversation ended up being a discussion on how she should never be embarrassed of getting the wrong answer, because I also get things wrong. I took the time to reassure her that a wrong answer just means a learning opportunity, and at the end of the day anyone that laughs at a person for getting the wrong answer is not a good person. There obviously was not a sudden miraculous change in my student, but I think by the end of the school year she realized that it was ok to not know the answer, give the wrong answer, but most of all still stay in class so that the correct answer was learned. The reason I took the time to speak with this student even though I was tired? I saw myself in her!

Another example of this that I have from a student, was early into the present school year. I was teaching an intervention class, and for whatever reason we started talking about grades and what school was like when students were remote. One student admitted that he did not go to school very much in the previous school year, and in fact would not log in for certain teachers compared to others. Most teachers would have taken this as an opportunity to tell the student about how important it was for them to log in and not miss school, but I again saw things differently. My first question to the student was "Why didn't you log into school for certain teachers compared to others, was it because you didn't like those teachers and didn't want to be in their class?" After the student answered yes, I asked him another question, "What made you not like those teachers, was it their demeanor or that you maybe felt they didn't care about you?" After a pause to gather his thoughts I assume, my student responded with "I just didn't feel like they cared, they didn't connect with us students…they just expected us to respect them and enjoy the subject even if we didn't get it. I didn't like that and it frustrated me so I just decided not to go to class!"

This isn't something that I'm making up to sell copies of this book, this isn't something that I over exaggerated, this is literally out of the mouth of a 7th grader that had to go through an entire school year on a laptop with a teacher he felt did not care about WHO he was. Some would say that the teacher needs to be trained on how to connect more with the student, others may say that the student was wrong for not showing up to class and the parents should have been notified and stepped up. I see it differently, what I see is a child who would rather the teacher love him and appreciate him even if his behavior is different. I see a child who is not being given new opportunities every day with the same content, that may lead to a lifelong passion for education in the future. I see a child that was comfortable enough to be completely honest with me, simply because I took the time to connect with the WHO rather than WHAT was within him.

Most of what I have been talking about so far can be summed up into one major theme that has led every year of my educational career. That theme is being able to see myself in my students, and be for them what I needed. This has led to my intentions of getting into the field of education, this has led to my pursuit of higher education, and this has also led to my desire to not leave the field despite the many experiences giving me a reason to leave. I don't know how to exactly help someone else understand what this means and how to go about always having this mindset in the classroom, but the best I can do is explain how I do this without having been trained on it. This was not something that I remember learning about in my undergraduate program. This was not something that I was taught when I was in student teaching, and this was not even something that some of the best teachers in the world speak to when they talk about their classroom methods. This is something that honestly I feel is an anointing on my life, a calling, a purpose that for whatever reason continues to keep me here.

Let me give you another example of how I connect cultures and make M.O.N.E.Y. in my classroom. The very first year I stepped into the classroom I was a young 24 years old, and pregnant with my son. I was super nervous, because I knew that I really didn't know what I was doing. The first couple of months I was graced with the ability to teach a sport that was pretty self-explanatory and not many directions were needed. However, when it came to basketball, there was a LOT that I had to explain and model before I could let students take part in a game. Therefore, I had to learn how to get the class quiet, determine a way to keep them all on task, and of course do it in a way that wouldn't seem like I was a military drill sergeant.

I could have used some internet suggestions, I could have even gone to other teachers that had more experience than me for ideas on what to do, but instead I sat down one day after work and thought about the previous interactions I had with students. After all of the ideas I had come up with, and ways to get students to "cooperate" during this sport, I chose to utilize music as a tool for classroom management. Now let me be clear, this was NOT the first time that music was used in this class, but it definitely was a chance to use the music in a different way than it had been before. Typically when music was used in this class it was with a lot of hesitancy. Most of the music that was put on was your typical pop music that had very little to no lyrics, random school house songs that have been recycled for decades on end, or kids bop. Even though these students were 9 or 10 at the oldest, none of them wanted to listen to kids bop for 40-45 minutes when they came to PE for motivation to participate. In fact, when kids bop was put on, most students would roll their eyes and laugh.

So one day I ran a little experiment in my class with these students. I found the edited (clean) version of some of the popular songs on the radio, and when students were entering into the class or working on individual skills, I would play them over the speakers. I didn't play these songs the entire time, but instead I would mix it up with the songs that were previously used as well. Keep in mind that back then this meant that I had to use different CDs, so it was not as easy of an experiment as I had hoped. Anyway, I noticed that when the songs from the radio were being played, students would be dancing and having fun while practicing skills. The minute the "old" music was played, students would start complaining and spend more time talking about the "lame music" instead of practicing the same skills they were having fun with before. What did this show me? What did I learn from this? Well, remember I said that when I think of or speak about culture, music is part of that. What this showed me is that the newer music I was playing was part of the culture of my students, and the "old" music that was played was not only a culture they didn't identify with, but it was also something that created frustration rather than motivation. The older music that was played was showing these students that they must adapt to this type of music during the class, even if it was a distraction to the learning environment. The other type of music being played, although something simple that most would not think about, was telling students "This is what I want you to enjoy even if this is not WHO you are outside of school."

You'll be happy to know that instead of going back and forth with the different music, I got to the point that I was looking up popular music all of the time, and creating CDs for students to listen to every time they came to class. I can remember some students even being shocked that I knew the music they enjoyed, and later claiming that I should've been a DJ instead of a PE teacher. I used the music as a way to get students motivated, connect with the class content, and to also see that even if I didn't 100% like the music they listened to, I was willing to have it in class so that it was a more enjoyable and motivational learning environment no matter what sport we were playing. It did not solve all of the classroom disruptions and distracting behaviors, but it did in fact decrease them on a great level.

As I close out this chapter, I hope that you have a very clear understanding of what the real money is in education. I hope you see what the real money in education SHOULD be, despite the many debates you have heard, articles that have been written, and comments teachers across the nation have given. Physical money does in fact help education in various ways, but on an individual level in the classroom, money does not do what we are really in need of right now in education. There are many students who come to us broken, or just in need of connection emotionally, and we must stop pushing it to the side hoping that new programs and procedures will be the solution to the problems. As society changes, the same should be seen and done in classrooms without hesitation or pushback. If there is hesitation or pushback, we must go back and remind ourselves of the purpose of education, and why our consumers (students) should be leading what we do, rather than professionals who may be out of touch with things in society. Students are not as uninformed as we have believed all these years. Students are also not "acting out" just to get attention from a lack of such at home all the time. What I really believe is happening in education right now is students screaming out and yelling to teachers in various ways that they need emotional connection and attention when it comes to learning. They are letting us know that the problem is not with the content within our classrooms, but instead the problem is with the method in how they learn. To be a viable citizen in society you have to learn to adjust and adapt when there is change and difficulty. How can we expect this from all of our students when they are older, if we are more concerned with the WHAT instead of the WHO and we are not taking the time to:

Make **N**ew **O**pportunities **E**very day for **Y**outh

CHAPTER 2

Time

Time is the one thing that I know for sure was not talked about in my teacher preparation program during college, and neither was the importance of managing time as a teacher. In fact, as I'm sure others can testify to, most of the classes taken in undergraduate programs across the nation are focused on lesson planning, understanding your content specific standards, classroom management, classroom rules and procedures, and who you should make sure you have a good relationship with on your campus. One of the books that just about every teacher has read or at least seen, when it comes to becoming a future teacher is "The First Days Of School by: Harry K. Wong". This is all important stuff to know and implement, but when is a 20 something year old going to understand how to manage time in the first few days of the school year? If you're a teacher like me or you know a teacher, then you know the answer to this is THEY WON'T!

The way that the U.S. collegiate system has trained many teachers like myself, is to go into the classroom, rely on what you learned in your college program, and you will be a master of it all in a few weeks if you're lucky. Maybe you laughed at that last sentence, or even shook your head, because you know that it's not the right way to go about teaching. This is why many of the teachers you know are frustrated and ready to quit between the 1st year and the 5th year. There is no possible way that an individual just getting out of college after completing 16 weeks of pre-service training, can command a classroom that will fully engage students and help them be successful in the future. Sometimes you do in fact see this miracle happen, but more often than not, teachers coming into the classroom don't have a clue on how to manage time in their new job, and there really isn't any effective mentorship happening in the first few years of becoming a teacher. As you can imagine, this has the greatest impact on students, and their ability to effectively learn and progress.

The time that teachers spend in the classroom and in the school itself is so overwhelming at times, that I have begun to believe it is the reason why so many of us have taken a serious look into leaving. Even though we enjoy helping students reach their goals, we have found that the old way of stuffing our needs to help others is NOT working anymore and needs to stop. Sadly, this old way of thinking and operating in education has created the foundation of education, which has led to so many teachers being overly strict in the classroom, taking more days off than normal, or even just flat out giving the bare minimum just to survive. When teachers have this revelation and begin to stop self-sacrificing, because of the long accepted culture of education, they are met with anger, push back, slander, threats, etc., much the same as students when they express their honest opinions about what is going on in education right now.

The time that teachers spend at work taking care of other people's children, being parents to neglected children, advocating for children who have been pushed through a system rather than helped, is something that is stripped from their own family. THIS is why TIME with family is so precious to teachers, but yet there continues to be more and more put on our plates with the expectation that we will just adjust and adapt rather than cry and demand change. One of the biggest examples of this is parent/teacher conferences. These conferences are important, but the logistics of these are not really what I believe they were intended to be. Across this nation, there are school districts that require teachers to stay at school as late as 7pm-7:30pm when it is time for conferences. When asked why they are required to stay this late, most administration will tell you it's because these parents can't get off work or come in earlier, and we need to be accommodating to these individuals.

From the outside looking in this sounds great and really empathetic. It sounds like the schools are really helping families to get the information they need no matter what their work schedule is. Sounds like the people who are with your child during the week for the most amount of time really care about you and want to make sure you don't have to stress…right? However, that's the view of those looking inside and not those who are inside looking out. Have you ever really considered how much neglect this is causing the child of the teacher to feel? From one single day of having to teach all day and do conferences all evening, that child probably only sees their parents for a TOTAL of an hour. Not to mention that when that parent gets home, they are exhausted, irritable, and maybe even cringing at the thought of having to get back up in less than twelve hours to do it again! I for one do not like these late conference days, and I would even go further to say I don't see the purpose of parent/teacher conferences as a whole in the field anymore. With all of the apps and online resources provided to families so that they can see their child's grade almost immediately after an assignment is completed, why do we need to set aside a whole week of ½ days?

On a personal level, TIME within education has been the one reason that I have gotten so close to leaving the field completely after fifteen years of service. Time for some individuals, when it comes to teachers, is just asking for an additional prep period, or a day off that won't be deducted from their PTO bank. To me, as you might already know by now, I see it much differently! Time is more than silence and no children in my classroom, and it's also more than an accumulation of a few hours that I can be away from the job! Let me explain it a little more for you!

When the quarantine of 2020-2021 happened, it honestly felt like parents and families were forced to sit and observe what all they never paid attention to in the past with their child's education. They had to sit down and take the TIME to see what it was that their student was learning, who the teacher was (personally), how other students behaved while in school, and most importantly the TIME it takes to really help a student to learn a new concept and later complete work to show mastery. Now don't get me wrong, not all teachers were enjoying doing their job online, because just like students some adults don't do well with being online. But what I and many other teachers thought would lead to more respect for teachers and the field overall, actually turned into more of a downward spiral.

When all this TIME was given to parents and families to truly engage in education, it was met with anger, rage, slander, threats, and even now, laws to put more work on teachers. Parents were given the TIME to see what it is that a teacher can do by themselves, but also what is truly needed from parents and families to help students get a holistic education. Instead of coming together collaboratively as a unit for the next generation, and understanding that families have a much more important role in whether their student succeeds or not, there was more pushback from parents and families, which to myself felt like a very sly way of showing that what level of respect I thought we had as teachers was even lower than we originally thought.

Time in education has become almost like a curse word, that when used to explain the internal fight to process through eight hours to an administrator, leads to a professional development plan or dismissal. Using the word TIME in education is just as irritating as hearing someone tell you to build in more self-care, but get angry when you go take care of yourself. Despite having gone through a pandemic and international quarantine, there are still individuals that refuse to allow real conversations to occur about what all of this has done to the mind of a teacher, or more importantly their child! Instead of conversations about how to improve the collaborative work that needs to be done in education, there has been more conflict and misplaced anger towards the very people that if not around would cause a major disruption in working America.

Parents and other stakeholders blame teachers for their child's learning gaps that have occurred over the last several school years. Parents blame teachers for their child being disengaged with the materials, even though for the last few school years they have had the freedom to game and go to school at the same time. Parents blame teachers for their child having self-esteem issues, not knowing how to communicate, not having a desire to interact with their friends, having low awareness of hygiene, the list could go on and on.

To anyone reading this who is not an actual certified teacher, know that the one problem I have with you placing blame on everyone else but yourself is that you don't recognize TIME is what has brought us here. The education system in the United States did not just crash and burn because of Covid-19 and the quarantine. The education system in the United States has been this way already for many decades, but many have not been listening or even trying to listen before responding to what you think is the truth. Many have not been listening to the teachers across the nation who have been advocating for change and begging that your level of engagement increase to a beneficial level for EVERYONE! What many have heard, and maybe what many have believed, is that all teachers want is more money to keep indoctrinating children every day, and making them feel bad because of what they don't know! If that's what many believe now, please get comfortable before you read the next paragraph, fill up your water, or whatever you need to do, because I need you to read this next paragraph with an open mind.

I don't mean to be so upfront and honest, but really if you take a step back, put this book down, and reflect on your own educational experience when you were in grade school, you could say you've seen these mistakes for decades. You have seen the teachers who got into this field for a paycheck and summers or holidays off with pay. You can remember the teachers who were verbally abusive to students, but when students tried to speak up for themselves they were made out to be liars. You can maybe even think of the times that you were much older and came to the realization that what your teachers taught you was good information, but also missing information that caused you to have learning gaps much later as an adult! In fact, I bet about 80%-90% of those of us who are no longer in grade school have more than a few traumatic situations we can remember from our past teachers. Not trauma like physical harm, but trauma in that it made you think MUCH differently about going and staying in school. We have all been there, and because of that, we need to stop acting like this is new information. Answer me this…who was your LEAST favorite teacher? Any doubt that there's another teacher in the classroom right now that is the same way but a different generation?

If you are just now reflecting on this and getting angry and ready to throw all of education away, you are late to the party. In fact you're so late that not even the police department is still around to investigate the noise complaint. They have figured out where it came from, why it was so disruptive, who was the first person to throw the water bottle to get everyone's attention, and the yellow caution tape is cut down and thrown away. You're so late that it's as if it never happened, and you're opening up an old can of worms and smelling up the place again. You're opening up a stink bomb and throwing it around angry, because you just heard everyone yelling and loud, but yet you're standing there alone in a vacant dance hall dressed up and fired up ALONE!

Do you get the picture? Is it clear enough for you right now? Are you beginning to understand why your current anger and complaints are actually irritating and disturbing to teachers and anyone connected to a school district? There is a lot going on in education right now, but it is nothing new. It is very old news that no one has paid attention to until they were forced to sit down and really utilize TIME to look at what's been happening within the realm of education. They were forced into the position of a teacher for their child an entire school year! Not to mention that arguing about it, placing blame on others for it, or even restricting teachers now in what they can and cannot do WILL NOT solve the issues!

Ok, let me give you another example of something that is happening now, but is old news and old arguments that have risen up. Just the other day, I was looking through my personal email, and noticed that I had apparently been added to an email list of a group emphasizing the importance of "parent voice" within education. This group's email, that I have no clue why it was sent to me, spoke about the fact that it was time for parents to "take over" education and "speak up" for what is right and what "they know is best" for their children, rather than letting lawmakers and teachers continue to do so. While this sounds nice and amazing and maybe even motivating, it is again people showing up to a vacant dance hall yelling and screaming at the walls after the event was shut down. Plus, if you know what is best for your students and what is best for teachers to do…why haven't you done anything about it until now? Why haven't you been a part of the committees and organizations that give you the ability to actually put words to action?

To the parents that argue about parent voice and advocacy, I'd like to ask you some more questions! When have parents EVER not had a right to speak up and advocate for their child's education? When have lawmakers EVER had a right to pass frivolous bills out of happenstance or random emotions, rather than answering to the community they represent? When has accountability of what and how teachers teach in the classroom EVER been regarded as a felony or misdemeanor? When have schools been able to secretly teach students controversial information, and place seeds of corruption in their brains so that they could be controlled and manipulated to do as the adult in the room sees fit? When have teachers EVER been allowed to act as they please, say what they please, and not be handed consequences for their actions whether the school agreed with it or not? NEVER!

I have been in the field of education for over a decade, and what I am seeing as time goes on is the fact that no one has really spent time within the field unless it is their career choice. The number one thing that time shows for the field of education, is that what has always been done is not the solution, but also the field of education has apparently been intentionally keeping stakeholders blinded and disconnected from what really matters until now.

The time away from in-person learning has shown us that there are various things we as a people have gotten comfortable with, used to, and let just fly on auto-pilot. We have let things slide and go by in the same way they did when we were younger, because we just knew that if we turned out okay, then it must mean it will do the same for millions of other young people. We have become a nation of complacency and dependency on others, without giving credit where it is due, or even remembering that at the end of the day it is all of our responsibility to educate the next generation safely and productively. That if they are not living as viable citizens of this country, it's not their fault solely, but it is ours as well…the previous generation no matter if we are the parent or teacher.

TIME

Time has shown that to be a student in the field of education right now, means that you are only allowed to learn rather than live. When students come into my classroom I always hear about their disconnection from teachers, because of the overwhelming amount of information they have to sit through. Students tell me all the time that lessons are too fast, and when they ask questions there is a sense of irritation rather than empathy to explain until students reach mastery. Ironically, this means that the field of education has become an entity that does not want to take time to help students to truly thrive, but instead quickly learn, gain, and master information so that they can move on to the next level of academics. This is ironic because while this is going on, we continue to emphasize and tell children that it's not about competition and speed when it comes to success.

Let's be realistic though, if time shows us that all teachers should be fired and all parents should be given the ability to control what goes on in the classroom, then what is the purpose of having teachers and education programs at all? If all parents know exactly what their students need, and the schools are just factories to produce students who have no ability to think critically or work without direct instruction, what is the point of having physical schools? Why isn't everyone online or being homeschooled by their parents and other family members? Heck, why not even go so far as to say we need to get rid of colleges and universities too, because parents have complete knowledge of the best way to build skills for the jobs their children want in the future?

Obviously I am being very sarcastic, but at the same time being truthful to combat the arguments that are going on in education right now. After all, some people argue that they are experts at various problems in the world, but don't realize that their solutions create further problems.

So what do we do? Why keep complaining and justifying whose fault it is? What are the first or next steps? Well the first thing, as I have been talking about this entire chapter, is looking at time. From my personal perspective I did not become a better teacher or develop a better culture in my classroom until I looked at what I spent most of my time doing in the classroom. If you were to take a look at what takes up the most time or what you do for most of the time, I believe it shows you a lot about the priorities you have as a teacher and a parent. This can also show you why your child or student doesn't respond to you when you've tried to do everything possible to connect and empower them!

Some of the best teachers I have had in the past did not spend all of the time in class teaching the academic objectives of the day. It wasn't that they were bad teachers or didn't know what they were doing, but instead it was actually because they realized, just like adults, children check out when either something is too long or something they can't relate to. So what did these teachers do? They would break up the lesson and make sure that as we were learning about the subject, we were also learning about ourselves, life, or even the teacher in a way that made it all make sense. This is a deeper conversation for another day, but just think about the difference you see in children that learn math through video game scenarios or their favorite things outside of school opposed to recitation and repetition. It of course takes time to figure this out, because all of your students aren't the same, but in the end it is definitely time well spent.

When it comes to parents, although I'm still learning this myself, it doesn't matter how long you've been in school, how many degrees you have or even if you have read a lot of books on how to connect and raise your child the best…you will still fail at some point. The same can be generalized into the field of education and what your child is learning now compared to what you learned when you were their age. What worked for you does not always work for your child, what seemed to make school fun and exciting for you is not the same now for youth. I have a teenage son right now and I can tell you definitely some days I drop the ball when it comes to my son learning, because he is not the same student that I am. Is it wrong that I admit that I don't know? Should I have kept that to myself? Does it mean that I'm a bad teacher because I can teach other children effectively but sometimes not my own? Of course not! What this means is that just like you I am human, and sometimes it's harder to loosen the apron strings with our own child than someone else's. What it also means is that we need to have more communication going between schools and home, unless we want to keep letting time go by and find more ways to justify that we aren't really seeking a solution.

Most of us think of time as something that we have to race to beat or rush to enjoy before it slips its way out of our life. Time, once you hit your 30s, is nothing that you intentionally take advantage of anymore, because you realize that you are closer to no longer living on this side of time compared to the other. However, time is something that if you really don't see the priority in and what you can do to invest in it more, you will see it as a playback of your mistakes, shortcomings, and faults when you are much older and cannot right your wrongs. So right now in education we need to make sure that we slow down and look at what time has really shown us? What has this playback, film, journal pages, or whatever you call it put right smack dab in our face as areas of needed and immediate attention before destruction? When we analyze our emotional reactions, our shifting preferences in the realm of education, what makes us uncomfortable to the point that we want to do SOMETHING to fix or change it? What feels like a red flag or red light shouting out loud "Look, look, look, over here!"?

Whatever was your answer right there is why you need to slow down and take time to really think about how you believe it can be solved. Education in the U.S. right now is a mess, I think we can all admit that and no one gets offended or appalled. But the fact still remains that it is not going to be changed or made better because of sporadic and impulsive decisions made by administration, superintendents, law makers, or even parents and teachers. To change education right now it takes intentionality, strategic methods, analysis of how we got here so we can avoid it again, student voices and feedback, more uncomfortable conversations, true parental and family engagement, but most of all TIME!

Time well spent is time invested and properly positioned for future change! Just like reading this book is something that you have to want to do in order to finish, the same can be said about what American Education should be. U.S. education for the younger generations should be something that they WANT to do because they see how it will empower them for the future, and help them to reach their goals and dreams. How do we get students to this point? How do we receive and take heed of their feedback and voices? That is the question of the hour, and it all starts with TAKING TIME!

CHAPTER 3

Dress Codes

When I first joined the field of education, fresh out of college, I was a physical education teacher. This meant that my "uniform" was athletic so that I could be fully involved in my classes. I was the only one on campus that dressed like I was always getting ready to go workout. Students for this reason always knew who I was and where I was. There were times that I would buy a certain pair of shoes or a specific shirt, because I knew it would get students talking or it would be a statement that I was "still cool" even though I was much older. I can remember the many comments of my family, who are now retired, about how I was so casual going to work and it fit my personality so well. I've never been the type of woman who spends hours getting ready because of having to put on make-up, heels, dresses, or anything like that. Even to write that makes me cringe because the few times I did dress up in front of my students they thought something was wrong with me. One of those times it was a bet that I had lost with a student in regards to exercise (pushups) and they told me I needed to "hurry up and get back to my usual…it was weird to see me dressed like the other teachers."

I laugh about this even though some could take offense, because what this lets me know is that students knew me on a deeper level than just their teacher…they knew who I was on the inside. Because they knew the heart I had for them and the career of being a teacher, they knew me in ways that maybe not even my coworkers knew, they knew that Ms. Armstead needed to go back casual and stop all this makeup, lipstick, and dress craziness! Even to this day, I ask my students what they would do if I showed up to work in a dress and heels, and they all say "Ask you what's wrong with you or are you sick?".

Even though this experience may be unique to me, it still makes me think about this whole concept of dress codes within education. Now first off, I'm not only talking about dress codes for adults, I'm also talking about dress codes for students. Dress code violations have become so high in some schools across the nation that they are changed and modified in real time rather than after the school year. In fact, I have been in school environments where students earn a detention or out of school suspension for not having a belt, or "violating" dress code more than a few times. I've seen schools try to combat these "violations" with incentives for not getting detention, paid dress down days, and even sometimes placements in newsletters to honor those who are "upholding the school's standards of excellence". The problem that I have with this is that it's missing the point. Putting all these things in place and trying to keep up with changing the handbook in regards to appropriate dress for students or even adults is treating the symptoms and not the root cause itself. I'm going to take a moment here and get really transparent with you about my health. But before you go further to read about it, PLEASE understand that there's a point to me sharing with you!

So most of my life I have been what you consider to be pretty athletic. I say pretty athletic, because while I always thought I was the best at any sport that I played, it was clear that my ultimate destiny was not to become a professional athlete on any type of level. I played sports a lot to pass the time, but I also tried to eat as healthy as I could once I was a little older too. I was never a person that loved to binge eat random food, try challenges of different concoctions of food, or go days on end without drinking water or whatever was a healthy alternative to pop (or soda for you west coast readers). I had my share of eating things and feeling the consequence of it later, but as I got older I noticed more and more that it would have a much longer lasting effect. One of those times was when I went to a new members event with a church that I used to attend. At the event there were your typical hotdogs (I won't eat unless it's beef), hamburgers, chips, pop, and for dessert ice cream with all the fixings. I wasn't really hungry for the food per se, so I took it upon myself to go ahead and get some ice cream. I know in detail now, because of the result of my consumption, that blue bell ice cream was not the best thing for me to eat at that time. Side note, do you remember when Blue Bell ice cream was being recalled because of a possibility of it having listeria? Yeah, well that was about the time that I was overconsuming this ice cream and toppings.

Anyway, I devoured my ice cream and almost immediately after, I felt that something was NOT ok. I was beginning to get nauseous and my stomach kept growing in size like I had a little munchkin making its way into the world. I stayed for about another hour or so, but soon I was begging my family to go home before I exploded. Once I was home that was exactly what happened…I was violently sick after eating the ice cream and at one point thought about going to the ER to be checked out. I didn't end up going to the ER in the long run, but after that day, no matter when I ate something I would have stomach pain behind it. I just took it as some residual impact from the ice cream, but speeding up a few years, it was hurting more and more.

January of 2020 I was trying again to shed some pounds off of me so I wouldn't be the typical fat PE teacher. Doing this didn't seem to take away the severe onset stomach pain I was having so I made it to the ER. When I was at the ER they told me that I had what was called diverticulosis, and if I didn't take my food consumption more seriously they would see me back in 6 months with a more severe problem. Let me stop right there and say that when a doctor tells you something like that, DO NOT take it as a joke, because almost 6 months to the day I was back in the ER, but this time I was barely able to walk, talk or speak because of all the pain that I had in my stomach. I was in the ER for all of about an hour or so after having a CT scan, when I was told by the doctor, that evening I would have to have emergency surgery or I would not make it another day!

What was the problem? Why did I have to have a 7 hour surgery followed by another surgery down the line? Well, this is where I get real honest and transparent…the surgery was required because when I had eaten the previous night, not thinking about what it was and just wanting to be full, it got into my digestive tract and got stuck within a pocket which is what diverticulosis is. Once it was in that pocket, it became infected and was not moving and passing through. So for two weeks I was at home enduring the pain thinking it was the same thing that had been going on for years, but eventually during that time it ruptured and sent all of what was in my digestive tract into my abdomen. Not only that, but I was on my way to being septic, infection going into my blood, and if that happened there was nothing else that could be done to help me to get better.

Prior to this I had never had any surgeries, broken bones, long-term hospital stays or anything….I was scared out of my mind! Apparently though, I took it on pretty well because everyone was shocked that I didn't want any pain killers or even break apart emotionally until I was laying on the operating table. I won't go into further detail, because this is not a medical discussion, but in total between those two surgeries I spent about 15 days in the hospital in 2020 during the quarantine and lockdown. I know this doesn't seem to have anything to do with dress codes or even education, but in fact it does!

All this time I was going back and forth to doctors, chiropractors, urgent cares and the like to see why my stomach was hurting so much. I was trying to drink more water, give up carbs (which I failed all the time with), exercise more, but it all never changed a thing. At the end of the day no matter what I did, I still had diverticulosis which eventually turned into diverticulitis, because of not taking care of the root cause over the symptoms. I was so busy trying to take care of the symptoms that I didn't really address what needed to be resolved so that it would no longer be an issue. I had to learn the hard way to pay attention to what I eat, how I eat, and how my body works, but we don't have to do the same thing in education when it comes to dress code violations....we don't have to continue learning the hard way!

Until I went through all of that pain and experienced those consequences to get diagnosed and find out what was REALLY going on, I didn't take it seriously and just believed that my age would save me. Much like myself, students don't understand the root cause of dress codes within schools, and some adults even display to them the lack of understanding of this as well.

Dress codes were never meant to be another method of controlling students or telling them what they can and cannot do. In fact, there was not a concern of dress codes until about 1969 when high school students took it upon themselves to oppose the Vietnam war in a very subtle way. During this time, it was the Supreme court that took it upon themselves to put laws and policies in place to avoid having another "disruption" to the learning environment by students. While I don't believe that students of today understand or even know that this was the reason for school dress codes initially, I do believe that they should be educated more on this along with what clothing choice says to others around you.

As you can probably tell by now, I have worked in different schools throughout my years in education. This was not because I didn't want to settle at a school, but instead because of the advice that I received many years ago to make sure I get a wide array of insight of what youth really need to succeed, instead of staying in one place for 30 years. For that reason, and to take heed of that advice, I made sure that I taught on just about all levels of education, and in all modalities. Through my time teaching online, in-person, charter, public, alternative and beyond I have seen and continue to see one thing that students need more education on, especially in light of the current ways of society! Students in this current season of life and society need more understanding and education in the area of self-respect and self-esteem.

During one of my classes that I had taught in the last few years, the topic of discussion was on respect. Without getting into too much detail about my discussion with my students on respect towards teachers, I want to zoom in on the conversation that I had with them about selfrespect and self-esteem. Whenever I would start to bring this topic up, most of my students would all of a sudden get quiet. Let me remind you that these were middle school students…it is very rare to get a whole class of middle school students to be quiet! Anyhow, I started this conversation with students to help them to realize that respect towards others is an important habit that will help them be successful, but even more important is having respect for yourself.

From that statement on, the conversation began to get really honest and humbling. I shared with my students that although it may not always be right, teachers judge and assume a lot about students based on how they carry themselves on campus. The way that you carry yourself isn't just your stride or whether you look up or walk with your head down. Those things are included, but the way that you carry yourself is also what clothes you wear, how you wear those clothes, what level of quality hygiene you have, etc. As you can imagine the eyes of my students started to widen and the questions they began to ask me revealed that light switches were being turned on. Students during this class discussion were realizing that the clothes they wore actually spoke to others before they opened their mouth up to speak.

I was able to have an honest conversation with students about the reason we have dress codes within schools. It's not that we as teachers want to tell them what they can and cannot wear (although some schools have uniforms), but instead we want to ensure that when students walk into the school setting, they are walking in confidence, security, and giving off the message that they do in fact love themselves and respect themselves. Dress code policies in schools to my students was all about control so they would wear things purposefully to rebel against this control as any teenager would do. However, once I taught them the root cause of the dress codes and what your outward appearance says to others, they began to understand that even beyond the classroom and high school, they want to be respected by others fully rather than judged for their clothing.

Now did this solve all of the problems with dress code? Of course not! But it sure was nice to see more than a few students walk into school with their own unique style, while also making sure that they no longer had to rebel against control. I can also remember that shortly after this lesson in class, I was talking with a few female students about the same topic. They were really struggling at the time with what attention males on campus were giving them or other female students based on the things that they wore or didn't wear. There were comments being made about them, because they appeared to be uncomfortable when they wore certain clothing on campus compared to others.

Of course as I was listening to this I could see myself in these students. I could see in my mind the many times that I was made fun of or picked on in grade school because I was NOT one to abide by the rules of my peers when it came to dressing a certain way or doing certain things. I was actively listening to them, but at the same time I was laughing in my mind because it was yet another time that I was reminded of the fact that what I went through as a child and young adult was with purpose. When I was their age I was always wondering what the purpose of my life was. Was I here just to be made fun of? Was I here just to constantly be told that I don't fit? Was I here just to look at life and fade into the background? So what did I say eventually? How did I respond when they looked at me for affirmation? Well, what I told them is:

"You are beautiful no matter what anyone else says. You will always have someone tell you that you don't look right or you need to change, but unless you feel it in your spirit, don't listen to people when they say that. If you keep changing every time someone says to change, you will be a hot mess living this life! I have always been told that I'm different, that I need to smile more, that I need to talk more, that I need to wear makeup, that I should dress up sometimes, that my standards are too high for a man to ever want to marry me, that I'm always going to be alone because I don't loosen up and you know what? I haven't changed AT ALL. I mean there's a lot I have changed as I've gotten older, but I have not changed from what I know I want, don't want, will tolerate, and will NOT tolerate. I always knew I wanted to be a mother, teacher, mentor, and I didn't allow ANYTHING to stop me from reaching those goals. Did I get hurt along the way? Did I get made fun of along the way? Did I get abandoned and disowned along the way? Yes, of course I did, but when you know who you are and what you want in life, that stuff doesn't hold you down all the time. When you know who you are you tend to move much differently than others. So don't worry about the clothes or the hair or whatever else, I am an introvert who loves teaching, reading, and reaching my goals. If anyone doesn't help me to thrive in those areas, their opinion of me doesn't really matter...does that make sense?"

I don't know if it was because no teacher had ever talked to them so up front and honest before or not, but the first thing one of the students said after that was "so you mean I don't have to wear skirts and dress up if I don't want to?" I didn't get angry or even try to answer back with another long winded response, I just simply said yes. That yes was a way of letting her know that yes if you don't want to do that...then don't! If you want to wear what's comfortable despite what others think about it...do it! I recognized that her question was more than just something to make me think she wasn't listening, it was a question as if to say, wow so I can be myself now?

It's ok to just be me?

So even though it was not intended at the time for me to talk about dress codes and why they didn't need to copy others just to be "cool", it was actually a conversation that helped this student to gain confidence and security in being themselves. I could only do this by being an example to the students I interacted with daily, and also be an example of someone that although others may not like or agree with, I still am myself no matter where I am, what I'm doing or what role I'm in. I was and will always be myself and talk about important topics with students on this level, because when it's all said and done, this is what they remember the most about school and take with them well into adulthood.

I feel like I may have gotten a little off topic when it comes to dress code, but the point I've been trying to make is that dress codes need to go back to what they initially started off as. Not controlling rules and policies. Not ways to subtly discriminate and segregate individuals across the school, but instead a means of making sure that students confidently and securely come on campus dressed not only to be successful, but with pride in who they are no matter who is around them or what is said. THIS to me is what the root cause of dress code violations with students is, they don't understand that clothing is a way of communicating with others, and often schools want to make sure that even when you don't quite know what you want to say, you at least say something that isn't going to destroy your reputation before you fully have one.

Now, I'm not quite done when it comes to dress codes, because it's not just students that have dress codes in schools, it's adults and even parents as well. The most irritating thing to me as I get older over the years is how much people judge professionals by what they wear or what their uniform is. I mean let's be honest, how many of you have seen the principal with a suit get more respect and appreciation than the parent who shows up in PJs to pick up their child after working a 12 hour night shift as an ER nurse? You may say, well that's because we don't know what the parent's job is and we are just seeing them show up to the school looking like they don't really care about what they have on! Or others may say, the principal has to dress up because that is how they gain respect, if they dressed down others wouldn't even know who they were or what they actually did at the school.

Excuse me while I roll my eyes at both of those responses! Really? Are you serious? So one person deserves more respect than the other and will get more respect than the other just because of how they dressed? That's the most foolish thing that I have heard of in all my years of education, and what's worse is that this is why I believe I have been and continue to be treated with less respect. Students over the years that I have taught have told me how their parents didn't want them in my class or their parents didn't want them to connect with me because of the way I looked or how I presented myself on campus. But on the other hand, I've also had parents visibly shocked when they meet me for the first time, because of the fact that their student was always talking about me and sharing how wonderful they felt on campus and in class when they were around me. Both of these situations make me laugh, but it's actually a serious problem in the field of education.

Why do clothes determine quality? I for one don't care what a person is wearing and care more about how they treat other people and make them feel. I have seen so many teachers come onto campus that are suited and booted (looking Easter Sunday ready) from head to toe, and yet they are the same teachers that students tell me they don't like. I have seen so many teachers walk onto campus looking like Starbucks, but on the inside and in the classroom their skills and cultural environment are more like gas station coffee (no knock to gas station coffee, I don't drink it, but you get what I mean).

The point here is that just like with anyone else in life, clothes do not determine quality. I drive home past some homeless individuals and I don't for once have the thought that they are all out on the streets by choice or addicts. I look at them as people who have had some bad cards dealt to them that they could not overcome. It's the same for the classroom, if a teacher is wearing jeans and joggers or heels and dresses, it does NOT mean that the joggers wearing teacher is trash. In fact, it could actually mean that students will love the casual teacher more than the dressed up one because they can relate more to that individual!

Now, don't get me wrong, I get the idea that as a teacher you want to look presentable and separate from students. You want families to know when they come into the classroom who

is who and the one in authority. But if I'm being real, when I did my doctoral research, and even

now when I ask my students…NO ONE CARES WHAT TEACHERS WEAR! Well, let me take that back, no one cares what teachers wear and the ones that do care don't really know what REAL teachers are in the first place if their outward appearance is the main focus.

In the last few years I have seen more and more articles on the internet asking questions about what parents would do if the adult in the classroom looked a certain way. Everything from tattoos, hair color, lifestyle choices and beyond have been used as a determining factor of the quality of the teacher. Sadly there are individuals that exist in this world who will not allow their child to be in a class with someone if they have tattoos or less than normal hair color. One thing I can remember someone saying is that teachers are setting an example to students, and that is why we should be even more mindful of how we present ourselves to students…after all if we don't look "up to par" we are letting students know that professionalism looks like me.

The problem here is that people forget that teachers are normal people in society as well. Although we have taken on the role of a teacher, we are still human beings that go home after work, stress about our children, take the weekends to detox from whatever went on all week at work, shop at the grocery store in crocs and sweats when we don't want to get dressed, have tattoos, different colored hair, have adult beverages on the weekends, and occasionally rage in traffic because slow drivers are all of a sudden on a mission to clog the streets. I mean what I'm trying to say is how can we hold such a high standard for what teachers wear or have, but at the same time pay them and respect them with so little potency that they in some sense are no higher than historic indentured servants? (No, I do not mean what you are thinking, if you don't know what an actual indentured servant is then PLEASE go look it up before you bubble up offense!)

Dress codes for teachers should be based on the position that the teacher holds within the school, but also on the demographic of students in the classroom. Just like language looks and is used differently depending on what community you go into, the same can be said about what individuals view when looking at clothes in the realm of professionalism. I'm not saying that dress codes should be completely thrown out, but when I look online and see a teacher similar to myself being blasted for wearing a hoodie, all I can do is shake my head. Some students would rather be in a classroom with a casually dressed teacher because they feel that it means they are more "real" and honest. However, in other communities, some students may feel like they will lose respect for a teacher that wears casual clothing and instead should be business casual. Some teachers feel more comfortable when they are able to dress down and focus completely on their interactions with students while they are teaching, while other teachers may feel like they are not their most confident in their role unless they are business casual.

Whatever the case may be, we need to understand that just like I told my students about clothing representing self-respect and self-esteem, give adults the chance to do the same! Stop pushing teammates (families and teachers) apart by focusing on something that has nothing to do with the end goal or intentions of schools being in existence in the first place. I for one don't even remember half of what my teachers in the past wore, because it was their attitude or method of teaching that I used to determine if they really did care about me and want to see me succeed in the future. If a teacher wore or had something about their personal appearance that I didn't agree with, it didn't make me lose respect for them, instead it helped me to realize that I have to look past what I can physically see and focus on what I can't see internally. It taught me that sometimes some people who look the most intimidating are actually the kindest hearted individuals you will ever come into contact with. It taught me that even when people do the same and judge me or assume things about me, I still need to be authentically myself so that others will see my heart instead.

Going to school or even working in environments where individuals were seen as "unprofessional" because of outward clothing made me actually want to leave the entity. This does not teach students important lessons about being okay with being yourself, but not always feeling the need to rebel or be so outwardly different to get attention and mask the insecurities you feel on the inside. If more students understood from teachers in the classroom that differences are welcomed, and we are not here to always teach academics but life as well...I bet we'd see less violations of dress codes. When you give today's youth clarity and understanding of root causes of policies and procedures, you will find less anger and frustration.

However, in education, the problem is and continues to be that most of us don't even know the root cause or the foundations of a lot of what we do and have done. Dress codes have been one of those things that should not be a war every time someone has a difference of opinion. If right now the focus is on closing the learning gaps and helping students to "catch up" after the nationwide lockdown, then how does what an individual wears distract or take away from that educational process? If it is not REAL a concern, then why did we carry it forth for so long? Can't we shift this and have more discussions on why students and adults should WANT to dress decently rather than dismiss the reasons they may not be with write ups and detentions?

I know, I know, wishful thinking is what some readers may believe this is, but as I continue to say...I see things much differently than the average teacher. Dress codes are one of those things that should be focused on intentionally to change rather than to tighten right now after all of that students and people in general have gone through. When everyone was online at home, there were a lot of things that usually would be a problem, but at the time were not a major concern. Truthfully, I believe they still should not be. Dress codes are one amongst many of those things, but sadly we continue to go back to what is comfortable.

CHAPTER 4

Educational Trauma

When I was a child I had some very traumatic experiences within education. I can remember being lied on by a teacher to my parents that got me in trouble, being made fun of and mocked by a teacher in front of a whole classroom, being ignored, and so many different traumatic situations that I could write a book alone on educational trauma and how it has a lasting impact on students and adults. When we look at education, not just the superintendents or the principals, but those who are at the top and making laws, we don't know what type of educational experiences these individuals had. We don't know if they had good teachers, we don't know if they had bad teachers. But just like a lot of people base their judgment and interactions towards others on consistent behavior seen, we could assume that the reason laws are being put in place and teachers are not getting the pay or respect they deserve, is because these individuals at the top did not have good experiences themselves when they were in grade school. As a result of their experiences, what ends up happening is when they are put in a position to impact the education system, they're not remembering the good things and the good qualities of teachers, they are remembering the traumatic, negative, and toxic experiences they had as children and basing their decisions off of the pain.

Some people would say, well maybe that is true, but that can't be possible for everyone because they have to be thinking about their own children in schools. What we have forgotten in this world and society, is that trauma replays in our minds like a tape. It plays over and over until we decide that we want to heal! Once we begin the healing process, it doesn't delete those memories of trauma, but what it does is guide us towards taking all the emotions attached to it, and producing something opposite of what those individuals did to us.

If you had a traumatic experience in education, or simply put you had some horrible teachers, you're not going to understand why teachers should be paid more, because in your eyes you're saying "We're going to give more money to the people who disrespected and abused me so that they can go around and abuse more children?". If you didn't have positive experiences in the classroom, you're not understanding why teachers should not be mandated to do extra work for children whose parents have not and will not step up. In your eyes you see it as "They knew what they were signing up for, they need to work, they need to do more training, they need to take more tests and have more professional development." That is all based on your true experiences whether they were good or bad.

When I talk about high school, I can remember one day especially in my junior year. I was getting so sick and tired of being bullied. I was always made fun of, a lot more in high school compared to middle school, for my voice. I was told that I sounded like a man, that I was too loud, that my voice was too raspy, that my voice was annoying and I needed to be quiet. So I decided one day, as a sixteen year old young woman, that I would not talk unless someone talked to me first.

When I got to school, I can remember not speaking the entire day. Now keep in mind, when I was in high school, school started at 7:15am and didn't let out until 2:10pm. I didn't walk to school, I didn't drive to school, I didn't get dropped off at school, I rode the bus to school. So you're talking from about 6:15a-6:30a to 2:10p or 2:30p, I did not speak a single word. I hope that shakes you from the inside out. I didn't speak a single word! No one called on me in class, no one spoke to me during passing time, no one wanted to have a conversation with me at lunch. Most people would be heartbroken if they heard that, and most students would decide that if this was one day of no one speaking to them, then why not speak again?

I could've taken that experience with me, that anger for feeling like Casper sort of speak, and decided that when I became a teacher I would retaliate. The reason why I didn't was because I realized that not every school is like that. Not every teacher is like that! Shortly after me not speaking for a whole entire day, there was a teacher in my keyboarding class, who decided to walk up to me and say "I've never really taken the time to get to know you, but I know there is something special about you. Tell me something unique about yourself that no one else knows." That teacher is one that I have remembered since being a junior in high school!

At some point, we have to get to the point of recognizing that the reason why education is the way that it is right now, is because adults who are connected to the field are not ,or have not, effectively dealt with the trauma that they have from their grade school experiences or even their personal lives growing up. Those negative experiences are sometimes triggered by current students who push a button unknowingly in the classroom or in public. Once they are triggered, it comes out in whatever way they release it, sometimes without warning or apparent reason but concluded in hurt and pain towards the receiver.

The only way that we are going to begin to change this within education, the only way we are going to shift this negative aspect of education and move forward so that we are competitive with other countries, is to recognize the severity of educational trauma, and the fact that this could be the reason why many students do not perform. Not just talking about it, recognizing it, and speaking up about it, but sitting down and effectively having conversations on how we can heal this! Out of all the things that we share with our students, we share this heavy weight of educational trauma. However, we are not teaching students the true life skills to release and heal from this educational trauma! We are just saying that this is part of education and it shouldn't be! Just because administrators don't always see this when they evaluated teachers doesn't mean that it is not going unnoticed.

Just like child abuse and neglect leaves a lifelong stain, so does educational trauma. I think if you've really read this book for any amount of time, you can see how the educational trauma that I experienced has stayed with me all my life starting from very young. We can't sit back and blame lawmakers, we can't sit back and blame toxic parents, we can't sit back and blame teachers, we have to recognize that none of this would be here if we all knew how to heal from our educational trauma. We also have to be proactive in preventing more trauma from occurring in classrooms across this nation presently.

One of the ways that I advocate to do that, which may very well be the reason that I have a target on my back all the time, is by letting students speak their truth without judgment! The reason why I'm not judging and I'm listening is because the only way that I can help others to heal in the way that I have, is by learning from their story! There's a lot of negative and toxicity that gets strengthened and empowered in schools daily when it is held as a secret and kept inside. Whenever you have the chance to speak your truth without judgment or criticism, it is healing from the moment you let it out. We should be offering this same opportunity every day to our students and even students on school campuses. I believe we would be surprised by what hearing the different transparent perspectives of others can do for school cultures and climates.

One of the first steps in healing myself from personal educational trauma and negative experiences was simply speaking out to a trusted individual these words:

" I experienced some very traumatic situations from teachers as a child. I did not speak about them because I was scared of what repercussions I would have from those adults. It made me feel inferior. It made me feel incompetent, and it made me want to disappear from the educational environment and life overall. It wasn't always from my peers, although they did bully and tease me severely to the point that I attempted suicide at twelve years old, but a lot of the trauma I experienced in education was from adults on my school campus..."

Those were some of the first words I spoke to heal myself from my educational trauma. I would suggest that you to do the same thing if this has brought up some past memories or pains from your school experience! Take the time after reading this chapter to admit that you have experienced some trauma in education, and call it what it is EDUCATIONAL TRAUMA! Stop stuffing it, stop hiding it, and speak it out! Even if you have to write it down...get that toxic stuff out of your heart!

Through your healing, try to help your students and student's parents heal from the same by letting them speak their truth with no judgement. When they ask you to speak or share your insight, help them to see it from a different narrative that is more positive, even though you can relate to the negative things that do in fact happen or have happened in the past. Share with them the things that are good! Make it your mission to find, speak, and share more of the positive things that teachers are doing across this nation every day. In fact, speak about those teachers that have really made a lasting positive impact on your life and why. I guarantee you it was not because of academics, and I can guarantee you that when you share positive after sharing your pains, it will bring more closeness to everyone you come into contact with both on campus and off. A major step in shifting the field of education to a more positive experience is understanding that although past habits and methods didn't work for all students, we can empower the future generations of students by not pretending that these things don't happen! Instead we can hear these things, process through these things, and use these things to make are more humanistic environment on school campuses across the nation.

CHAPTER 5

Trust

Trust isn't just this complex word that a lot of people use to cause you to shiver if you don't have it with them. Sometimes trust has been used as a tool to get people under someone's control, but that doesn't work in education, and that's not what I am talking about in this chapter. Trust within the field of education isn't something that you can just develop after having the same work environment for many years. It isn't even something that a lot of people realize they have lost over time. Why? Because trust is something silent, soft, and simple, but unfortunately in the field of education, it is being broken whether intentionally or not.

If you ask any teacher in the field right now that has a little bit of seasoning to their career, they will tell you that the one thing that was good about remote learning, was the fact that there was more autonomy and freedom to just teach. Students were still being taught academically what was required, they were still being given assistance with homework and projects, but what was different was classroom observations and documentation. While online, teachers didn't have to worry about a random and unannounced visit from the principal or assistant principal to see they were doing their job. There were no walkthroughs by coworkers to come and sit and unload all of their emotions and gossip on you at the end of the day, when you were really trying to sit in silence before having to go home. There were no calls to your classroom to check and see if you did attendance, or if you had your grades up to date. At that time in the 2020-2021 school year, the major concern was to make sure that students were learning and showing up to class with the best teacher for them at the time. There wasn't a push for a new program and policy. There were no complaints about the environment of the classroom, because the classroom was the home environment!

To me it meant that there was a lot more trust in teachers during that time! The focus of everyone at the time was to make sure that content was given and students had someone consistent to speak to even if just for a few hours. There wasn't a focus on how much you interacted with coworkers or attended events on campus to "make yourself a part of the school family". No one was going to the principal or whomever on campus to spread gossip and possibly lie about why someone did something or should be reprimanded. There wasn't a feeling of a gray cloud when teachers were starting their day with students, even if it was a difficult learning concept to teach. I don't know about you, those who were teachers online during that time, but to me I felt like I had more trust and was trusted more by administration and coworkers! The only thing that I had to do was focus on making the online learning environment fun for my students, so that they could do well academically despite all of the craziness in the world at the time.

I can remember when I needed to get to some appointments, I didn't have to jump through hoops! I was just told "adjust your schedule as you need and let your students know". I was able to get to where I needed and not worry about PTO being depleted. At another time, I had to figure out how I was going to get my son to his state testing, while also having to prepare my students online for their state testing the following week. I was given the ability to teach "on the go", which meant I was in my car waiting for my son outside, but teaching my students according to the normal schedule. I made sure to let my students know that I was in my car, but that it was going to change nothing! I utilized my hotspot on my phone to teach them all subjects, answer all their questions, and even hold additional office hours! It was amazing that I was able to have a "normal" life of being a single parent and teacher, but also being trusted that I was going to do just as well outside of the classroom with no explanation needed. I was trusted, I was appreciated, I was seen, and I was heard, but between that time and the present…it is not the same situation.

Since being back in person, I have felt as a teacher that I am the punching bag and pin cushion for all frustrations whether my fault or not. I have had parents accuse me of indoctrinating their children because I am teaching about social emotional content. I have had individuals question what I do during my prep periods throughout the day. Heck, I have even had coworkers go and complain that I have "too much time" and they are not sure that I'm using it to actually plan, but am instead just browsing the internet or whatever false narrative they had in their minds to push. For that reason, I was always asked to take on other roles within the school environment when "no one else" was available to do it. I was asked to do just about every job you could think of…even being the school nurse!

As you can imagine, I was very frustrated and at times angry, so much that all I could do was keep reminding myself that it wasn't about me…it was about the students! Now understand that I'm not putting all this information here to get pity or some type of empathy. The reason I'm including this is so that you can feel the same frustration and anger, and you can also understand what it genuinely feels like to NOT be trusted as a teacher. To not be trusted as a teacher in this current society means that you are treated very similarly to students. You have so many rules and regulations, that it feels almost like you are accused of committing a crime even before you had the thought cross your mind of what that action was. I have heard of teachers being asked to wear body cameras, post their lesson plans publicly before teaching, explain why a child is "bored" in class and parents believe they are not teaching, etc. The list can go on and on, but the sad thing about the list is that if you're not a teacher or know a teacher, you would probably believe that all of these things are made up and fabricated.

When it comes to trust for teachers, and the field of education as a whole, what some people don't recognize is that when we were online, that was when the field was forced to trust the ones teaching students. There was no excuse! No one could come to their house, no one could come and force them to be evaluated...you HAD to trust the individuals who were teaching students. There were first year teachers during online learning, and they may not have had the skills that they should have, but the administration had to trust that whoever they hired was going to do the right thing. They had to fully believe in their hiring practices, and believe that these individuals who had never taught before were going to teach students effectively throughout remote learning.

Now that we have gone back to in-person learning, it's almost like people have forgotten how much teachers, who were online, could be trusted. It was like all of a sudden everyone was saying "I don't trust you anymore!". Even though we were online and were able to teach 30 to 40 students or however many students without direct help and connection from other people, all of a sudden with no reason we couldn't be trusted.

At what point did teachers show that we cannot be trusted? People are screaming indoctrination, people are screaming critical race theory, people are screaming all these other vulgar things towards teachers right now. However, there's no detailed explanation on where they are getting the information from that says all teachers are doing such hateful, disgusting, inappropriate, and violating things in the classroom with students. I'd like to believe that the reason a lot of people are saying this is because of a small group of teachers that have violated law or policy, and now that it's exposed, the comfortable and easiest thing to do is to say that ALL teachers are that way.

I've seen plenty of articles and statements online with social media that say all teachers should be treated like law enforcement and wear body cameras. The thought behind this is that law enforcement wears body cameras due to the current climate of the U.S. society, and cannot be fully trusted when giving testimony of what actually occurred. There are two ways to look at this, one this is true! There's too many people dying at the hands of officers, not just people of color, so we need to have some way of monitoring what they are doing. If they turn off their body camera, then we know that they can't be trusted. The other way of looking at this is, as a lot of people say, just because a few people are bad doesn't mean that everybody is bad. So if you start making it like everyone is bad and everyone can't be trusted, what you're going to have is a lot of those that CAN be trusted leaving. There's a reason why certain individuals left service industry jobs during the quarantine. Look at how many nurses decided that they would all together leave the field! Consider the amount of nurses that decided that they would rather become traveling nurses instead of being on staff at a particular hospital! No one wants to be treated like they can't be trusted when they haven't done anything!

This same concept can be seen with a spouse, child, or even a student since we are talking about education. When a student is in the classroom and they are being controlled by everything, that student is going to rebel by doing things that get them out of the classroom. It may be getting a suspension, getting a detention, it may even be something as simple as constantly asking to go to the bathroom, nurse or seeing the school counselor. This is because the student feels like they are being treated as though they are a prisoner or criminal, even though they have done nothing wrong.

I believe this is exactly how a lot of teachers feel right now in education. There are some teachers that are taking a lot of PTO days to the point that they are depleting all of it because they don't want to be at the school. There are some teachers that just do the bare minimum, because they feel that if they are treated as if they aren't doing the best that they can do anyway, why take the time to go above and beyond only to be exhausted, burned out, and still told it's not enough?

What's happening right now within education is a whole mass of individuals who are doing amazing things in the classroom, now being treated like the few who are messing things up for the rest of us. If you really sit and think honestly with yourself, you remember as a student and child, a situation with your classmates or siblings where you all got punished because of something that one or a few others did. You remember how angry that made you feel, you remember how frustrated you were because you knew that you literally had nothing to do with it. You were raging mad because you had to deal with the consequences that should have only been dealt to others, but the adult in the room felt that everyone was in trouble, because if one person did it that meant all did it. We are trained as teachers to not punish a whole class for something that a few students do, so why is society doing this same thing to teachers?

I think the main problem or the main thing that happened when everyone was remote was that the eyes of parents were fully opened, as I mentioned in a previous chapter. The eyes of parents were open and they began to see what was actually happening with their child when it came to education. Across this nation, as a result of that, some teachers were exposed. Some teachers were exposed for what they weren't doing, and maybe some parents saw that the teachers in that particular school weren't doing what they should've been doing. They saw some teachers laying down in bed trying to teach, they saw some teachers being extremely controlling and rude and demeaning to their child. They saw some teachers who weren't helping or holding office hours, leaving their child to basically fend for themselves in that environment. But parents that saw that believed it was how ALL teachers were. Subsequently they jumped to conclusions and said very slanderous things before recognizing it was just THOSE teachers and not EVERYONE! Once it was said and put out into the world, trust was broken, and we are where we stand right now.

There are so many times in education that trust is violated! Once trust is violated, just like in any other relationship, it is very hard to be able to get back. I have been in education for a long time, and in this current year that I'm teaching, this is the least trusted I have ever felt. I feel like because no one is trusting teachers all of a sudden,

I am always overly self-conscious about what it is that I do in the classroom. I over analyze everything that I do, everything that I say, everything that I don't say or do, everything that I'm using to teach, everything that I show students, every conversation that I have with parents and students and coworkers, everything that I post in my own social media and my own life, I over analyze it because I do not feel like I'm trusted. That is the worst feeling in the world, because I have not done anything to cause that.

I have been a passionate and very personable teacher. I've always let my students know that I'm here for more than academics. I'm not here just to teach so that they can get a grade in my class. I'm here to help them realize who they are, what beauty and royalty they have, so that when they get out into the world as an adult and they're my age, they take the skills that I've taught and do better than me. But even though I know that's what I'm doing, and that's what I'm about, it's not what the world is saying right now! So everything that I do, I have to over analyze it and I have to prove myself to the same people who trusted me fully only two years ago.

That's why teachers are beginning to leave! That's why teachers are beginning to hold back on doing what they've always done. We feel like we've gotten to the point that if someone is going to say that we're doing something we're not, we are tired of having to prove ourselves! We are tired of having to prove ourselves to parents, administration, and even legislators that don't even take the time to visit schools to see what's actually going on. We're tired of people in high governmental positions pushing a narrative that is false, disgusting, and is hurting education as a whole. So instead of fighting, instead of constantly saying the same things we have said for many years and decades, we're just deciding to stop! But then when we stop and we don't want to do half as much as we used to, people still find it in their hearts to complain! They still complain and say "oh look that teacher isn't doing anything, and that's exactly why we are doing this!" Or some will say "oh look that teacher is so quiet now, they used to be so energetic! Why? What are they doing behind closed doors to students?" It all makes for a very solid level of distrust!

Sadly in education you have people saying they don't trust teachers, because teachers are being incarcerated for things they are doing to children. You see teachers who are reacting inappropriately when a child is screaming at them or whatever the situation or context may be. Yes, there are teachers out there that are doing those things and should absolutely be removed, but that's not ALL teachers! The reason why everyone is jumping to believe that, is because they don't have trust…they haven't built trust over time, and everything that triggers them is made out to be what the heart of EVERY teacher is!

So how do we build trust over time? What are some of the things that we need to do? We can start by looking at our relationships! When you are building trust with someone, it starts with the amount of time that you spend with them and what you see when you watch and observe them for a while. You don't get in a relationship, well you don't get in a mature relationship, and automatically trust this person with your life when you've only met them two weeks ago or started dating two months ago. There's a difference between two weeks and two months! You ask deeper questions so that you can build more understanding. When you're dating somebody you want to make sure that they don't have residual trauma that's going to come out on you when you trigger them unknowingly.

We should do the same thing in education, we should allow time and environments for parents and teachers to ask questions. Questions like "what was your educational experience like before you became a teacher?", "why did you REALLY become a teacher outside of wanting to help children to learn?", "why do you continue to teach even though all of this is going on within the field of education?". Asking in depth questions like this allows for ALL the people connected to the children to have a REAL conversation. That's how you build trust. I'm not going to ask someone I have been dating for two years what their favorite color is. After two years, knowing your favorite color is not going to mean anything to me. I'm not going to ask a teacher when I first meet them in depth questions either, but once my child has been in that classroom for two months or more, I'm going to start asking deeper questions because I have a right as a parent to really get an understanding of who this person is!

A lot of people would say you shouldn't want to give all of your personal information to the parents you are connected with in the school, because you don't know them and they are strangers. Well, that is one of the major problems…we shouldn't be strangers! If your child has been going to a school for a significant amount of time, why are you afraid to ask some of these questions and have these types of conversations with teachers and administrators? You should know them well by now…they should know you!

I don't know why we forget that the school environment and home environment only thrive on how well we build a relationship. Right now it's clear to see that there's no trust in this relationship! When you're in a romantic relationship and there's no trust, you can get out of that relationship, you can break that relationship off and say " you know what, this doesn't seem right to me". However, you cannot break the home environment from education. Children have to be educated, children have to learn, and they have to learn effectively. So if we can't separate the relationship between education and home, then what is the solution?

We have to learn how to fix it….we HAVE to fix this relationship! When you're married and you get frustrated at your spouse, you don't just up and leave. You don't just all of a sudden call it done, because you can't stand the way your husband or your wife acts when they come home from work or when dealing with something tedious…you have to work it out…you have to figure it out!

We NEED to start building trust! We build trust by spending time with each other, by really listening to each other, by going through things in life with each other, by understanding the other person! We build trust by giving people grace even when it doesn't make sense. We build trust by taking time to process our thoughts and emotions when something frustrates us, then going back in a respectful way to appropriately address it and have a conversation to reach an understanding.

I know this may sound so simple and "stupid" but it's true! Education has turned into an environment that pushes the support system away, for fear that if they are closely connected we will be exposed because of something negative! However, IF there are negative things that are being exposed or eventually seen, that means it needs to be exposed for the good of change!

Trust is huge, and we don't have that in education right now! Teachers don't trust the families, families don't trust the teachers, legislators don't trust teachers, and we don't trust them! Yet we keep rocking on this boat as though there is no water that's sinking us in the back, and as though this is not impacting students. When there is no trust between adults, there sure as heck is no trust with students either. When students do not feel trusted, as I've already mentioned, they will find every way to avoid the relationship and leave. This is what students are showing right now by not being engaged with their work, by not wanting to do athletics, by not wanting to go to school, by not staying in the classroom, by displaying behaviors like selfharming and suicidal ideologies. All of this is happening because there is no trust whether that is between the student and teacher, or the student and their family! They don't believe that the people standing in front and around them every day truly love them and care about them as a person more than their academic grades. Until we get back to that, until we start emphasizing trust and pushing that more and expecting it of ALL teachers and adults, we're not going to see any good things happen. IT ALL STARTS WITH TRUST!

These are just a few of the simple ways I've seen over the years to build trust not only as a professional teacher, but as a student myself in the past. We can solve this! However, the longer we take to really work to start this and solve it means that it is no longer that "we don't know what's going on", it's that we don't want to do the work, we don't want to put our boots on the ground, WE want to continue to be a part of the problem and not the solution…so it's time to build TRUST!

CHAPTER 6

Students

If you've been paying attention to the text for any amount of time, or this is the first chapter that you have read in my book, you should know that students are the most important thing to me in education. You may think, "well, that's obvious, you're a teacher and students are supposed to be the most important thing", but it's deeper than that! I didn't get into education for the accolades, for the awards, and for the attention. I didn't get into education to get to a high position to be able to control different things. I got into education because of the many experiences I had as a student that made me want to give up. I got into education because of the many experiences that made me not want to pursue higher education. I got into education because of the many experiences that made me search within and believe for many many years that there was something wrong with me!

STUDENTS

Every single student that I see, that I've worked with either past or present, I see as young kings and queens. I've had people say to me "why do you keep calling them that? They're not all young kings and queens, you should just call them by their name." That's the problem! I've worked with youth that I don't even know their name. I've worked with youth in various environments, some of them I might have talked to just in passing in a grocery store, and I see young people as young kings and queens, because as adults we are kings and queens. There may be things that we went through in our lives that led us to believe that's not what we were or what we are, but we are kings and queens. We are all put on this earth for a unique purpose that only we can fulfill. THAT ultimately is why I got into education, because I realized as I got older, those experiences I went through, that no one else has gone through, were leading me to my calling in education. Students need someone daily in the classroom to help them to discover the same thing, but at a younger age so that they are motivated to do well in school despite setbacks. I saw a meme not too long ago from a very prominent individual, it could've even been Martin Luther King Jr., where it says "that which angers you, frustrates you, and presses on you as a burning need that must be met, is the area in which you are to lead." When I read that for the first time it resonated with me, it confirmed that yet again teaching is in fact my calling. But when I say teaching is my calling, a lot of people have this misperception that because it is my calling it has been easy. It has actually been the hardest thing that I have ever dealt with in my life. I have gone through divorce, I've gone through some ailments, I've gone through being illegally laid off, I've gone through not being selected because I didn't "talk myself up enough", I've gone through a lot of difficult things in my life, but the one thing that has been the hardest is teaching. It's not because of the students, it's because when I look at what students have to go through, how some students are treated, how some students aren't given opportunities to successfully break generational curses and do what they were put on this earth to do, I can't sit there and tolerate it! That passion of mine is why I believe it's been such a tough time!

When I look at students, I don't just see young people or young adults, I see myself! There are some situations where I've had students that I can't relate to or I wasn't in their specific situation, but in general I believe the reason I connect with many students is because I see myself in them and they know it. Instead of looking at them as a person that needs to be fixed or a person that needs to learn, I look at them as THIS IS ME...WHAT WOULD I WANT SOMEONE TO TELL ME OR TEACH ME OR GUIDE ME IN IF I WAS IN THEIR SHOES?

More recently, the one thing that I'm reminded of every time I see students is how difficult it must be to process things that are going on in this world right now. When I was a teenager, I didn't have to deal with social media, we barely had cell phones. I didn't officially get my own cell phone until I was paying for it myself, and that was maybe back in 2000 or 2001. I was a senior in high school or just graduated! I had the typical brick Nokia cell phone where you had to go and buy the minutes. If you sent a text message, it not only took you a while to send it, but it counted towards your total minutes. So if you bought 30 minutes and sent ten text messages, that meant that you only had 20 minutes left if you actually wanted to make a phone call. Wow, talk about real patience and budgeting right?

So anyway, I grew up in a day and age where we really weren't big on text messages, social media, and cell phones. Most of what we did was personal interaction! We had to talk to each other face to face. If we had issues with somebody, we either faced them or we avoided them and acted like we didn't know what was going on. When you watched the news and you saw all the things that were going on, you were able to find somebody to talk to and actually engage with. You were able to write things down and process through them. I was an adult when 9/11 happened! To this day I can still see exactly where I was when it happened. I was able to sit and talk with my family about it and the emotions that I was feeling about it all.

It's not like that right now for youth! Youth don't always have the ability to sit and have a conversation like that with someone. I mean, they have others they can talk to, but society has changed so much, and it's almost awkward for them to be face to face speaking about authentic emotions. The way that they talk to each other is through text ,or through social media, or very impersonal ways. So when I go into the classroom, because that's always in the back of my mind, I'm reminded of how important it is for me to show these young kings and queens that I love them first before anything, and that it's okay to

DIFFERENT and DEFICIENT

be human and express authentic emotions and feelings without fear or judgment.

I think that's probably the reason why so many students love coming to my classes, because they know that when they come to my class, even if they are having a horrible day and are being rude and disrespectful to me, I'm not going to return that. Even if they are embarrassed by it or shy afterwards, I'm still going to be there for them and love them anyway. I don't do that because I want to get all the students in the world to love me and be popular. I do that because there are so many children in classrooms right now that go home and don't have anyone to really talk to without judgment or a lecture. They don't have any way of appropriately expressing what's going on inside, and it's my job to be a living example.

This is why students to me are younger versions of myself and where I could have been. If every time I was in the classroom I made it look like I had it all together and didn't identify with them at all, there wouldn't be any reason for me to be shocked when my students didn't respect me. I mean, be real, who wants to be around someone who never admits that they got things wrong or were in trouble a lot as a child?

I've had many students over the years. I started working with students and teaching in 2006, but if I were to count my student teaching it would be 2005. Over all these years I have seen students in some very very scary situations that I could never imagine being put in. Most of those experiences that stuck with me the most, and trained me to be a very empathetic and personable teacher, are when I was working at an alternative school. I mention this all the time, but at this alternative school, these students when initially coming to the school already felt worthless and defeated. They knew that they were kicked out of the general education school setting to an environment where you are seen continuously as different. They don't have their friends around them, no one usually comes to the school to visit them, it's like they're isolated!

They are already feeling defeated and like nobody cares! It's scary!

When I first got there, all that I saw were these very angry children. I won't even sugarcoat it, I saw things like spitting on teachers, throwing chairs and desks, cursing teachers out, scratching teachers...anything you could imagine a child doing when they are at their wit's end! Keep in mind that I never worked for an alternative school before, I was never in this type of environment as a student, and I was scared along with feeling incompetent! Again, I have always seen students as younger versions of myself, so when I looked at these students I just tried to be nice, because although I believe I would've been in an alternative school if there had been one, I always craved kindness from adults. I tried to get to know them! I know that when I was a kid, when I used to haul off and get upset at my teachers, sometimes it was just because they just weren't listening or they talked down to me as if I was a toddler. I can remember being angry because some of my teachers were treating me as though they were perfect, and I was this imperfect individual that was inferior and needed to "just listen to them" for everything I needed.

I couldn't stand feeling that way!

So when I first met these students at the alternative school I started to focus on being personable. I started talking about video games and TV shows. Most of the students at the time were wearing Chuck Taylors, so I started buying Chuck Taylors myself with different colors and different styles. When I would go to work, my shoes would strike up a conversation! I remember one time, I had some shoes on (pumas) and my students were laughing, because it was so hot here in Arizona that I stood still too long while I was teaching outside and my shoes started melting below my feet on the asphalt. They were laughing, and I could see that some of them were trying to hide their laugh because they may have been thinking that if they laughed out loud it would lead to trouble…that bothered me! So I started laughing along with them, and letting them see that it was ok and normal to find it funny! I laughed to show them that it WAS funny, that it WAS ok to laugh, and it wasn't disrespectful to me. I wanted them to see that if they would laugh at home or with friends, then don't be ashamed to do it in school. Sadly I think they were afraid because there are so many teachers that take laughing personally, and then respond with aggression because they feel disrespected. I'll never understand that though, because even when I was teaching PE I would tell my students they could laugh anytime I made a fool of myself, as long as they knew I was ok first.

Anyway, I continued to chop it up with the students, and I even started talking about music with them. I knew we didn't listen to the exact same music (I'm an 80s baby), but since when does music NOT bring people together? I would find out the music they were listening to, check it out when I was at home, and then play the edited version for them while they were in class sometimes. I did a dance unit based on their music choices at the time. A dance unit with alternative school children! Everyone else at the time was thinking, "how in the world are you going to get these children to dance...they don't want to dance!"

Most children in general education settings don't want to dance and I knew it, but I told myself and I told others, we will do it! At the time shuffling was the popular dance, and I found other dances that were popular through social media to teach them. Why? Because I knew that if I was in their shoes, I wouldn't want to learn square dancing or ballroom dancing, I wanted to learn the dances that were popular and were what everyone else my age was doing! Even though it was uncomfortable to me (I'm not the best at these new dances), I know they had fun and could also see that I cared enough about them to find dances they enjoyed more than me.

Another thing I did was take the time to sit down and think about ways I could motivate them to work hard. My Mom and I are thrifters and often spend the weekends going to various stores looking for deals. One time I went with my Mom to a couple different thrift stores, and there were these rubber duckies, small rubber duckies that you typically put in the bathtub when you have a little baby or in a kiddie swimming pool in the backyard. I started thinking, what can I do with these rubber ducks? Eventually after a few days a vision came to me and I thought: What happens when you put a rubber duck in water? Even though you push it to the side or you try to sink it, it pops right back up in the water…it always floats and never sinks. So that's what I decided to do with the ducks!

I ended up putting my name on each of the ducks, and I would have my students work hard to accomplish something! I don't remember what I specifically had them do, but anytime that they accomplished this goal I gave them a duck. On the bottom of the duck I would take a sharpie, and write a message to them on how proud I was of them to be encouraged to keep going. I was proud of them because even with their setbacks, they kept going and working hard! I don't know how many of those students still have those ducks, but I hope that at least one of them kept it.

I can even remember when fashion bracelets were super popular. The bracelets where you take the strings and you put them together, almost like friendship bracelets when I was a child. The colors of the school I believe were green and white. So, I took from pop culture (these bracelets that were all the rave at the time), and when I knew I wasn't going to be returning to the school after a professional promotion, I took the bracelets and handed them out to each of the students I was working with. They were so happy, because these students don't normally get gifts or get things freely without having to earn it. When I gave them these bracelets, I had one for myself as well, I told them "these are our colors and I want you to wear this, so that anytime you get mad or upset, or you feel like no one loves you, I want you to look down at this bracelet and you remember us here and know that you are not alone, and know that you ARE loved!"

There may be even more things that I did while I was at this school like that, but the biggest thing that I remember is starting up sports. The reason why I remember this most is because when I initially started it or wanted to do it, people were against it. A lot of people thought that it would be impossible to have students from an alternative school compete in sports without getting angry or getting into fights with other athletes from general education schools. However, when I have a vision of something or I want to do something, I have a tendency of just going along with it until it is completed. Initially I started off saying we could do track. Track is an individual sport, you don't have to come into contact with anyone, and if they don't meet the expectations that I set for them then they will be off the team. I have found that when you set high expectations for children, and you couple that with true love and respect, they will do whatever it is to work hard and meet that goal if it's what they want to work towards! They work hard because they want to accomplish the goal, but more importantly they don't want to let you down!

That's exactly what happened! I started off with a lot of boys on the track team, and eventually a lot of them fell off because of whatever shortcomings that they experienced. I ended up having about four or five students go with me to the district track meet from this alternative school. I believe in the end it was about two or three of them that placed and ended up coming back to the school with medals from events they placed in! Although they were proud, they did not understand or know how proud I was more than them. I was SO proud of them, because these were students that came from an environment where they were constantly getting detentions, suspensions, getting in trouble, but were able to go compete on a district level in a sport where they could get medals! Not only that, but it would always be in the records that they were able to do that while in an alternative school! In my pride for them, I made a little book with all of their pictures and encouraging words so that they could continue being proud that they were the inaugural sports team of this school! Again, I don't know if any of them still have this book, but

I hope that at least one of them does! I hope that as they reflect on it, they continue to realize how much I cared about them.

Those are the things that I did for those students, and that pushed me to do those types of things for all students. My thoughts were, if that's what worked for students who are already "behind", then why wouldn't it work for students who are already on benchmark and already on track? Any school that I have gone to I don't see students as someone that I need to teach, someone that I need to change, someone that I have more education than, or someone that I am better than. I see them as younger versions of myself! I always put myself in their shoes, because I never know how I could've been in that same situation. If I was not blessed with two parents who strived to get their college education and break generational curses in their families, I could be in the same situations as these individuals. In fact, in some instances I WAS in the same situation as some of these students, but they don't believe it because of the way that I am now. I never want students to think that who I am now is who I've always been…that's not empowering.

There are so many teachers right now that give this image to students that who they are now is who they have always been. They don't share their educational experience, they don't share their childhood, they don't share their humanity and all the things that are going on. That is why I believe students don't connect with them! That's why students show discipline problems, because again that goes back to trust! I can't trust you if all that you're doing is sitting up here lying to me and acting as though you're perfect!

I don't ever want to give off that image to my students or ANYONE that I talk to! People think that because I have a doctorate I am this super intelligent person. I may be smart, but at the end of the day I still struggle! I still have to go to Google, I still have to look things up! And when you know that you're not the only one that struggles, goes through hard times, and it's okay to ask for help and get it wrong, that's something empowering…that's why I have no shame in my game to share that with others! At least for me it's empowering, because it shows that it's okay, that I'm not the only one going through this, that there are other people out here going through the same type of things, and I can get through just like they are getting through it too!

Students to me are more important than even the title of students. Student means you're striving to learn something, and sometimes I think that people seem to forget that students can teach teachers. There's a lot that I have learned from my students, not just cool pop culture things, but I've learned a lot about what it really means to educate the next generation and what are some of the best ways to do it. To me, students are not just students, they are consumers!

When you're a consumer you have power to dictate what is coming to you! You have the power to decide what you will and won't put your money towards. You have the power to change, turn, and shift the economy when you have money and are consuming products. So if students are consumers of education, that means that they have the power to do the same thing within the educational system. However, a lot of people may say, if that's the case why don't we see that power within students being recognized and used? We don't see that, because education has grown into an entity that now wants to keep the student voice quiet. There is a fear that if students speak up, there will be things that change that make adults uncomfortable. But just like in the regular economy, we don't have the same televisions that we did 10 years ago, we don't have the same cars that we did 5 years ago. Why? Because consumers want difference, they want change, they want efficiency, and as life changes you have to change things. If you don't change, no one will buy what you are offering, no one will have anything to do with it…it will be a waste of time and money!

When it comes to education, students aka consumers should have that same power! We should not be looking at education and seeing the same things being taught, the same things being done, the same things being restricted, the same things being slandered 20, 40, 50 years later. As life changes and society changes, consumers change, students change! Is education going to change every single year like cellphones? No, but should it change every 3-5 years?

Yes! Why? Because things in the world change! What I do right now in 2022 is not the same as

2019. If I take something from 2019 in a car and try to implement it in a 2022 car, it won't work! In education we need to take this same concept and apply it immediately! Students are not just students! Students are consumers with power, they have a LOT of power! We as the adults in the system should welcome their insight and power, we should NOT be striving for changes and answers without asking our consumers who are directly experiencing the system!

While we keep stifling their power and pushing student voices away from the system that is supposed to be preparing them for the future, we are doing a disservice to them when they get into the real world. When they get into the real world and into college, they don't know how to make decisions, they don't know how to give feedback, they don't know how to advocate, because they have been trained since kindergarten that you do what you're told even if you see things differently that could be better. They are trained in many ways that their creativity and feedback is a problem! Just look at the various reasons that students get marked down on project based learning assignments!

In my classroom most of the time, students give me more feedback than I give them. When something is boring, I ask them! If they don't like it or I need to switch it up, that is exactly what I do! What I have found by doing that is that students come into my classroom, even when they are having a bad day, and they feel empowered because they have a voice and they can use their voice! I should be embodying the concept of it being an honor for me to teach them, not for them to be in my classroom!

When people are given power, the only ones that abuse their power are the ones that are insecure and think that power means respect. Your level of respect isn't determined by how much power you have, it's by how you treat other people, especially those you feel can't help you in any way. So if I'm teaching students that they have power and they have a voice, the best thing I can do is let students know that I need their help, and they are the ones to tell me. When I do that through my respect and true care for them, when I teach or go to make changes, I'm going to see immediate success, because it comes from the mouths of those who are sitting in the classroom wanting to give feedback on what will work best for them. It shows them that teachers are trying to teach according to the way that they learn, rather than forcibly getting students to learn the way that teachers teach.

If I was an organization like education and I wanted to make money to stay in business, I wouldn't continue to neglect my consumers. I would make sure that my consumers are the number one individuals I'm listening to and getting feedback from on a consistent basis. This is the only way to make sure that whatever I do is going to make an immediate positive change, and it will be the right thing to bring me more success to survive in the current society.

So again, students are not just students, students are consumers and we need to continue to see them as consumers, because how is it that they are a part of a system that's meant for them, but they can't talk and give feedback about the system and its performance towards them?

If we give students more of a chance to utilize their voice, to see the power within them, and to use that power, what we will find is that the things we have been fighting to change over decades and centuries in education have simple solutions. From students in my classes to students across the globe, if we really dig in and pay attention to what they are saying on social media or day to day conversations in the school setting, we'd see that a lot of their solutions don't involve money! They don't involve major changes! What it does involve is starting with making sure that all teachers get to know their students on a deeper level and be more HUMAN in front of them. My students know all about the many shortcomings I've had when I was in grade school. They know how I was in the principal's office, how I didn't play sports because of my insecurities, how I was NOT a straight A student and was in fact a C average student. My students know that, and understand through it that I am human! So when I make mistakes in front of them when I'm teaching, or I seem to be a little quiet and sleepy one day, they don't anticipate that I am going to take it out on them. They know that just like them I just need a little grace and space for the day! They know that I am HUMAN and experience life the same as them, but I am here to guide them to appropriate expressions of emotions through trial and error sometimes.

The more that people begin to realize that students are more than students, and we owe it to them to get and utilize their feedback on a consistent basis, that is when we will begin to see things truly change for the better in education. That's when we will begin to see students who are actively engaged in their education, that's when we will begin to see students take more ownership of their performance in the classroom. When you give students more power and more responsibility, what you will end up seeing is more motivation and more attention to the process that they are going through in education. The opposite of that is happening right now in education, because there are so many adults in the field who are trying to change things based on what they remember in their own educational experiences, and negating the fact that our experiences are nothing like the current experiences and perceptions of current students.

The only way that we are going to know and have a deeper idea of what their experiences are, is to ask them and listen more than we respond! The question I always have as an educator, especially right now after having lived through a pandemic and remote learning, is as a field of education why are we so scared to ask for student feedback? Why is student feedback not included in teacher evaluations? What is the worst that can happen if we get that feedback? Would it be something that makes us cringe…maybe! Would it be something that makes us angry because it was based on assumptions…maybe! Would it be something that makes us angry because we didn't know or see that this was going on or being done…maybe! But what if getting that true, authentic, and consistent feedback from students was the answer to all the change that we seek right now in education? What if getting that feedback helped us to see ourselves through a mirror instead of rose colored glasses? What if that feedback was a come to Jesus experience for the entire field so that there was more accountability and quality control based on the consumers of the product instead of the higher positioned individuals who over time have lost sight of what education really is about?

CHAPTER 7

Administration

In the last chapter I ended with a short mention of the words quality control, that we must have quality control within education. Well, when you look at education, there are individuals in the field that are considered to be in the role of quality control. Quality control, even if you do a simple google search, gives you an understanding of what their true job is. Their job is to make sure that products being produced or sold, meet the expectations of the consumers. As I mentioned before, students are not just students, they are consumers and are consuming the things that we put out into the educational system. The tricky part about that is sometimes those are quality things and products that we are giving these students, but other times they are not. The bigger question here though is…where in education have we ever seen, heard, or read what the expectations of the consumers are…our students? When have we been able to sit down and see what the expectations are of students, and the type of learning environment they want to get?

Now let me first say this, because I know a lot of people may have this in their thoughts as they read this, I am not saying that you ask preschool or kindergarten aged students what their expectations are. Obviously, they don't know what the word expectation is, or what it is that they expect for adults to do in the classroom. Most of them would probably say to be nice, kind, etc. What I'm talking about is learning the expectations of our consumers from the time that they are in 5th through 12th grade. At that age students have already gone from being young adults and knowing the rules and policies without question, to now actually seeing and knowing whether something is helpful to them or a trigger of discouragement academically.

The individuals who are in these quality control positions, obviously administration, need to understand the importance of consumer feedback and how it leads to quality at the end of the school year. The first thing they should be reminded of is the understanding that their job is primarily on making sure that what is being presented or given to our consumers meets their expectations! Some of the other things that I have found in regards to quality control, when I was doing some reading myself, are that the job of quality control individuals is to test and assess products, monitor the quality aspects of the incoming materials to the organization, and the outgoing products. In other words, they are looking at the individuals and tools that are going to be used to develop and create this successful student at the end of the school year.

So what does this all mean and what am I trying to get at? Number one, administration in my eyes and many other teacher's eyes is not to control and micromanage in the school. They are not put in that position to tell adults, grown adults, how to do their job or how they should behave when they are not at their job (social media). Administration is not there to teach a teacher how to teach, an administrator is in that role to monitor, advise, and to guide the individual (the raw material/the building blocks) so that it can reach the students in a quality manner, and they (students) become viable citizens of society. That may sound like a lot, but what it basically means is that administrators should not lose sight that they are on the same playing field of the teachers in the classroom.

All administrators at one time were classroom teachers. They were in what some of us call the "trenches" with students. They had to do the daily lesson plans, they had to gather data and read the data, go to professional development, while also trying to balance their own personal life. They had at one point, a clear understanding of what it meant to be a teacher in today's society. When they decided to go higher towards becoming an administrator, they had to go back to school, pass a test, and then have this displayed on their certification that they were "qualified" to be an administrator. If you understand my train of thought, you understand that the method of becoming an administrator is a problem. The only difference between that person and those still in the classroom is more education and text on their certification. They DIDN'T gather more quality, they DIDN'T gather more power, they DIDN'T gather more respect just by getting more education and passing a test. None of these things truly define or display the heart of this person for education and its consumers (students). Essentially what it says is that they passed a test that was the method of determining if a person is qualified or not, that their ability to take tests or write papers "well" was good enough to be an administrator, along with their time in the classroom.

Another thing we have to think about when it comes to administrators is that title doesn't mean knowledge. A true administrator is a person who is looking outside of themselves in a way that will help them to become better within themselves. A true administrator is a person that can look at themselves and where things are not always right, and then make themselves better because of feedback from others. A true administrator is also someone who's main goal is to develop and create other leaders besides themselves.

The reason why this is especially important in education, is because an administrator is the main person in the school for quality control. They are trying to make sure that what's being produced or presented to the consumer meets their expectations. If you're only focused on yourself as an administrator or keeping like-minded people around, you're forgetting that some of the teachers you have are doing a wonderful job, but just not doing it the way YOU want it to be done. There also may be teachers on your campus that have "defects" and are not doing the right thing, but because they are like friends to you, you are more hesitant to have constructive conversations with them for the benefit of students and their quality education.

One of the best administrators that I have ever had was when I was working at the alternative school. To be completely honest, that alternative school was one of the most life changing experiences for me as a teacher. Not because of the type of school that it was, but because of the training that I received. I was going for my own masters in educational leadership when I worked at this school, so this administrator I'm about to talk about was like an in-house internship without the technicalities that we all know about! This individual at the school was someone that I should've known was fully committed to being on my side from the very beginning. I went through the interview, I went through the whole process and I was at the point in which they called my references. I got a call from this administrator, and they asked if I could come into the office and have a short chat with them. Of course I was scared and wondering what this meant, because this had never happened to me before. In the past, either I got the job I had applied for or I didn't.

So I went and talked with this administrator, and they started off the conversation with "Do you know why one of your references might have said that they would not rehire you?". I remember taking a deep breath and explaining to them that I knew exactly who would have said this and the reason why. In the end the administrator said it all didn't really matter to them. What they wanted to know was the truth, because in spite of that they knew that "the best educators sometimes have to endure the worst treatment, because others don't know how they do what they do so well."

I could've cried because I had never been in contact with an administrator like that before, and to this day I can't say that I have ever again. I have had some good administrators over these years, but I have also had some really bad administrators as well. This was one of the best ones that I ever had! This administrator giving me that chance was also why I continued to sign my contract …I felt trusted, appreciated, and seen! THAT is a true administrator focused on quality control. You're not just looking at a one-time situation, or listening to gossip about a person, but you have enough conversations and observations to know that despite this teacher doing something different, they are the best for the job of providing a quality education to the expectations of the consumers (students).

So that was the best administrator that I had ever had, the worst administrator that I ever had was probably when I was first starting out in education. I had started out teaching in a school that was K-5th grade. I was fresh out of college, and I started off teaching with another teacher. About the 2nd quarter or 3rd quarter, the other PE teacher had decided to take an extended leave of absence. Prior to this, this individual kept going to the principal and saying false things about me. Saying that I was being too lenient with the students, that I was playing music that was inappropriate because it was music students were listening to on the radio, that I was trying to do too much and not giving the other teacher a chance to "share the load". So anyways, this individual decided to take an extended leave of absence after having some surgeries and different things going on. It was then just me and a substitute teacher.

What most don't understand about this school situation is that class sizes were HUGE! They weren't just 35-40 students in each class, there were multiple classes in the gym at one time. There were classes as large as 88 students in the gym. You can imagine how difficult it is to have 88 students within an elementary sized gym! I definitely got training quickly on planning and creativity through this experience! If I wasn't prepared prior to this, I definitely was going to get prepared and master it so that students had the best experience possible. This is probably the reason why large classes and loud students don't bother me as much as other teachers…I had almost 100 at a time every day with every class in my first year of teaching!

Long story short, I go through the entire school year teaching these large classes with just myself and a substitute. At the end of the year I found myself in the administrator's office. At the time, you would go to the administrator's office to find out if you had gotten your contract renewed for the next school year. So I'm sitting in this office, nervous already because of how the school year went, and I'm waiting and hoping to hear good news. However, the conversation starts off with the administrator talking about how they feel that I thought I was better than the other teacher because of where I was born. I didn't respond and the conversation went on to my contract not being renewed because " You don't fit here! You don't fit in education, and I would suggest that you think about going back to school to find a different career." As you can imagine, I wanted to quit at that moment. I wanted to be done, I never wanted to teach again, I never wanted to be involved in education, but for some reason I felt the push to stay. That was the worst administrator I ever had, so when people ask me about administration, I like to tell them I've had both extremes.

The irony of this though, is that the administrator that told me I don't fit in education is now no longer in education after spending their entire administrative career at one school in the same role...they never did anything other than the same job! However, the administrator that gave me a chance, after hearing negative from my reference, was removed from being an administrator. If you think about it, who should've been the one between the two to stay an administrator? Hopefully you are thinking of the one that gave me a chance! Why? Because that person has the heart and understanding of what their job is as an administrator. Their job is to examine, observe, advise, guide, and as a very last resort dismiss when something is not being done correctly on a continuous basis. The focus should not be on you having to look, talk, act, think like me, and if you don't you don't fit here and need to leave!

Administrators are supposed to be looking at the incoming and outgoing "products" of the school rather than the teacher themselves. In other words, if a student enters into the school with a lot of baggage but leaves the school empowered and successful, then the machinery that helped that to happen (the teacher), should be sustained! Sometimes what we find in education is administrators that forget the focus is not on them, and the method is looked at more than the end product (empowered and successful student), and if it doesn't match who they are as an administrator they are let go!

I have experienced this for maybe 90% of my time in education. Many people like what I do for students. They love the connections I make, they love the engagement and respect I get, but they don't like the method in how I do it. They don't like that I'm not aggressive and I'm not assertive, that I'm not controlling or giving off an image of perfection to my students. They don't like the way that I'm personable and human to my students. They don't like the way that I learn my students. I learn about the community that they live in, I go to their events outside of school. I communicate with their parents apart from academics and discipline…they just like the end product (empowered and successful students). But they don't like the quality of the machinery (myself) that got the end product. I am also not the only one that has experienced this!

There are many other teachers that feel the same way right now! I've heard many teachers say "why are you so focused on my personality and how much I'm engaging with other people, rather than the proficiency that I have to produce quality students?" I've also heard other teachers say "When students come in my class you don't hear a lot of yelling and screaming or disrespect, and it's not because I'm controlling them, but it's because they know that I love them and want to see the best in them, while working hard at the same time to reach success!" I don't do things by everyone else's method. I don't walk to the same rhythm as everyone else. Sadly, as a result of me being "different" I have been seen as deficient. I have had plenty of administrators push me out, rather than trying to figure out what it is that I do to get students to succeed, despite it not being a traditional method.

Teachers do not leave schools and districts solely because of the pay, class sizes, school environment, or even the commute to work. Teachers leave because of administration. We want to know that the person at the top isn't focused only on who I am as a person, but rather on how they can get the teacher that has the "secret sauce" for student success to spread that throughout the school environment. Teachers also want to know that no matter the method of teaching, as long as it's in alignment with standards and the law, they have the freedom to be themselves while doing so. This is the reason why so many public school teachers make the decision sometimes to go to charter schools. Most charter schools don't have such strict rules on how a teacher can teach. They are allowed to be more authentic and creative, to get students engaged in their learning. One of the best examples of this is Ron Clark Academy!

Until we get administrators to understand this whole concept of quality control, we will continue to have teachers leaving. Teachers don't leave schools…they leave administrators. Administrators should not be dictators, they should be individuals who focus daily on quality control. If it works…keep it! If it creates defects….adjust and correct. If it works and it's unique…determine ways to sustain and spread!

CHAPTER 8

Teamwork

Teachers are about as important in the field of education as breath is in the lungs of a human being. But in this chapter, I don't want to just talk about how great teachers are, and give people another text to read that says why they should respect teachers more. I think in the last few years we've heard enough and seen enough of that. What I want to talk about is the fact that people in this U.S. society have begun to see teachers from a skewed point of view.

I can remember when I was going to school in the 80s and 90s that teachers were highly respected. The respect wasn't equal to the amount that they were getting paid, but there was a lot more respect for teachers. I spent my kindergarten through 3rd grade school experience in a catholic school back in Michigan. At this catholic school my teachers were all nuns. Now, just because they were nuns didn't mean that I respected them more, but there was more respect because they also had to display an equal amount of respect to children as they did themselves. I didn't have perfect experiences at this school, I did experience some trauma in 3rd grade. However, for the most part, students knew that when their teacher was talking or asked them to do something, you were not to talk back or be disrespectful because there were consequences. Whether that was what we called hard labor, which was going out and cleaning up the school campus, or staying after school to have a conference with your parents, students knew at that time that teachers were to be respected.

When I was going to school, teachers would call your parents even before you got home, so you knew as a child, if you got in trouble in school it would be double that amount of trouble when you finally got home. Not only did parents hear about what you did in school while they were at work, but now they had to come home and deal with it after being in traffic or even having a bad day at work.

That's one of the first things that I feel society has shifted in with education. Teachers are now seen as these individuals who are supposed to be superheroes. Initially when people called teachers superheroes it was nice and kind, but what we didn't think about is the fact that superheroes are also people that have to hide their true identity. If you notice every superhero that you see on tv or read in a book or comic has some type of mask. They cannot be seen, whether it is Spiderman, batman, or wonder woman there is always some type of mask or way to hide. Why? Because their true identity, their true selves can't be revealed or else others would discredit them despite the good work that they do. I believe this is what has happened in education in regards to teachers.

There are so many things that are being put onto the backs of teachers right now, but at the same time we are expected as teachers to keep our true selves out of it. We're not supposed to show how we're stressed out, we're not supposed to show how we're hurt by the words our students or parents have said, we're not supposed to show that we have a regular life. We can't show that on the weekends we like to travel with our families, binge watch television, we like to fall off of the grid for a little bit and not be seen or heard. Or one of the biggest controversial things that I see now is, some of us are adults and like to have adult drinks!

What's happening is when teachers nowadays begin to reveal their true selves by being more personable or honest with the stakeholders in education, there is anger that comes back. Now there are individuals (adults) that feel like knowing a teacher on a more personal level will lessen the level of competence this individual has in the classroom. That because they know about their personal life outside of school, their perception will then change towards being more negative. That's a shame! Whether you know the teacher on a personal level or not, it shouldn't have anything to do with what you think that teacher's professional skills are. That is one of the first things that I find is heartbreaking with teachers and the way that we are seen right now in society. We are seen as these individuals that are supposed to go into the classroom, take what little we're given, and create miracles, go above and beyond, fill in where parents and families have decided they don't want to do, and we're not supposed to show our true selves or be human. We're just supposed to just keep doing the job! Hello society, we are not masked superheroes...we are humans with emotions and feelings just like others in fields of knowledge!

The next thing that I see has changed with teachers in the field of education over the years since I was a teacher and even when I first started teaching, is this concept of expertise. There are a lot of individuals that may get a masters, doctorate, national board certification, become an administrator or superintendent, or school board member that are then called an expert. This term has been thrown around and used loosely in education for many years! A lot of people are told that they are an expert or highly qualified teacher, and others think that when this is attached to a teacher it means that they know everything. While some individuals may in fact actually know in depth all there is to know about education, others cannot fully show this sense of expertise. Despite me having a doctorate in education, I am not what I would consider an educational expert....I am an expert in the areas that I have spent a lot of time studying and researching.

I have a doctorate in education, but I am not considered an expert in education in that I know all there is to know about education. I'm an expert in only a few areas. Those areas for me are organizational leadership, organizational development, parental engagement, student engagement, parental and student advocacy, classroom management and culture, etc. These areas of expertise for me are NOT the answers to all things education. There are people who ask me about curriculum or finance, and then they get frustrated or try to throw negative words at me when I don't have the answers for all of that. That's not just my experience, there are teachers that don't have the doctorate, masters, national board certification, and are certified in the field with an expectation from society that they are supposed to know all there is to know in education. I have actually sat in rooms with parents and teachers where the parents get mad at the teacher because they don't know the solution to get their child actively engaged in the educational environment. This teacher may be wonderful at everything that they do, but this one student is their challenge. Parents and other adults assume that because the teacher is not able to resolve this situation then that person is not a good educator.

Teachers are not experts at all things education, they are experts in specific areas that build on and grow along with other teachers' areas of expertise within the school. If you take anybody from any field of knowledge, from nursing to engineering, to IT, to aviation, to whatever you want to think about, that person is not an expert in all things of that field. There are a lot of people that walk around in society and call themselves experts, but they are not experts. Experts are not people that know all things about that subject, experts are people that know all things in depth about a specific area within the field. Because teachers now are being called these experts, highly qualified, and any other loosely thrown around term, I believe that is the reason why a lot of adults are now advocating for a lot of the dysfunction within education. There are adults that believe that if a teacher does or says something incorrect, they did it intentionally because they should've already known. Teachers get things incorrect because they are not experts! Teachers are teaching and doing things within the classroom based on what they know, and what they have individual areas of expertise in.

When I sat on the school board in my local school district about a year ago, a lot of people used that term with me. They said that "Dr. Armstead is an expert in the field of education!" While it may be nice when people put titles and words on you like that, I didn't really like that mantle put on my shoulders, because to be an expert is not to be an expert in all things within that field. To be an expert means there is a specific area of knowledge that you have studied, and you can speak in depth about this as well as guide others in the study of it for an extended amount of time. An expert is someone that not only knows a lot of information, but it's almost like they are an authority figure within that specific area of knowledge or they have some type of authoritative knowledge. So when I sat on the school board and individuals were calling me an expert in the field of education, they were in a sense saying that I have authoritative knowledge within all areas in regards to education. That is not exactly true!

When it comes to my time on the school board, I entered onto the school board so that I could take the advocacy work that I was doing in the classroom onto a bigger level. I wanted other educators and other individuals to see what I do in my classroom to get successful results, and they could take that and spread it to be a leader on their own. I was not trying to get onto the school board to say that I had authoritative knowledge in education and everything that I said or suggested is the way that we should all go! When I make suggestions in the school environment, or even the things that I write in this book, it is based on my individual and specific areas of expertise. If another teacher were to write a book about the realities of education, and their area of expertise is curriculum and instruction or special education, it is going to be totally different! We may share some trains of thought, but they are not all going to be the same because we're not experts in the same area.

The last thing that I wish people understood more about teachers, and how it's changed, is that we are in fact a part of a team. We are part of a team! Right now we are missing our teammates! If you imagine just for a second that you're on a basketball team, and you're on the court and your coach is sitting on the side. Side note, coaches shouldn't be coaching players as the game is going on while they are on the court, they should've been coached enough to be able to coach themselves on the court! Anyways, the coach is on the sideline, your team is on the court, and you're in the middle of a game. There's supposed to be five players in a game of basketball, but let's say that you're missing two and you only have three. You have a point guard and a shooting guard. If you know anything about basketball, you know that this wouldn't work because you need a center so they can keep the other team out of the paint, and you need another guard to play solid defense as well.

That's what's happening in education right now…we are missing teammates! In education you have the teacher, the student, the parents, and the administration. If you're missing the student, or the student is not engaged, you can't be successful as a teacher because the whole point of being a teacher is to teach the next generation. If the parent is missing, you're not going to be successful as a teacher because if the parent is missing you don't have the teammate that's going to help to carry forth the motivation and empowering of the student to see the purpose of education. If the administrator is missing, you're not going to be successful as a teacher because you don't have the support of the school environment to be able to do what you need to do.

Obviously if the teacher is missing then we have a huge problem!

So we have four teammates, we have the teacher, the student, the parents, and the administration. Right now as a society in the U.S. we are missing the parents and the administrator the most. In schools right now, what we are seeing is that the only true teammates that are present are the teacher and the students. If the teacher gets burned out (which is what we're seeing a lot of right now) and they don't have the solutions to help the students, the student is the only one that the teacher can get the feedback from. If you're thinking about this, then you see that this is a major problem, because most students don't know all the time what they need. I have already talked about how they can provide feedback, but that feedback must be collectively looked at and utilized between adults. When we don't have those other adults and stakeholders to bring together for this, the system is then just between the teacher and the student...dysfunctional.

In education you see that there are teachers against students and students against teachers, meaning that there is a wall, there's conflict, there's disservices happening every day! There are teachers that are trying to go into the classroom and teach, but there are students being disruptive, because they are still dealing with trauma from dealing with the pandemic and national quarantine or other things. In years prior, the teacher could reach out to the parent and get support, but now the teacher can't reach out to the parent because the parent is still struggling to get back above and stay above water. The teacher also can't go to the administrator, because the administrator is not supporting the teacher because they are focused on whatever is going on right now on the government level of education. So we went from a four part team to a two part team!

I know a lot of people will use the example of a stool that has a certain amount of legs, and if one of them is missing then it will fall. I have heard it a million times, as I'm sure you have too, and it doesn't excite me when someone shares it. So instead of that, I want you to think about the four chambers of your heart. You have to have all four chambers of your heart working to stay alive. If you don't have all four chambers in your heart, let's say one of them gets blocked or clogged, you're not going to be able to successfully live life. So what happens when one of the chambers doesn't work? They do a bypass surgery or place some type of device to assist you with functioning properly. However, if it gets to the point that those things don't work, then eventually you're looking at needing to get your house in order because your time is short.

Similarly, we are looking at the same thing in education right now. We are looking at only two chambers in the heart of education working properly...the teachers and the students. Although people are saying that students are behind, they're not achieving success, there are in fact students that are working really hard right now! In fact, there are a lot of students working really hard, because they remember what it was like to be at home online and how much they missed being at school in person. Despite these chambers working, we have two other chambers that are blocked! We've tried solutions, we've tried putting in a pacemaker which was all this no child left behind so that we could try to get everyone on track. We've tried bypasses, we've tried to give everyone money in hopes that more money would allow us to get these resources and find success, but those things aren't working! So just like when individuals have their heart chambers functioning improperly, the doctors will typically say we have tried everything, and there's nothing else we can do. They also tell you a certain amount of time that they project you have left to live.

In education we have tried many solutions and methods to try and get the heart pumping and working correctly again. We have tried these different things like curriculum, character education, state assessments, district assessments, etc. However, in a sense we are all saying there's nothing else we can do. Sometimes, what you find when people have heart issues, blood pressure issues, or cholesterol issues is that the doctor will tell them "YOU have to get your diet right! YOU have to actively make the choice that you want to live, you want to be healthy and that you want to change! If YOU don't want to, there's nothing else that we can do!" So in education right now, I feel like that is what we are being told. We are being told that as a U.S. education system WE have to want to change! WE have to want to be healthy, WE have to want to survive, and there's nothing else that anyone else can do. Because the government has tried everything, other entities have tried everything and it's not changing. Why is it not changing? Because of the fact that teachers are being seen as these experts, superheroes, and the only ones that can bring success to students.

Until we get back to realizing that we are a four part team, and we all need to come together and start off slow/small and build on that, we will continue to be an unhealthy two chamber heart trying to function. We will continue trying to compensate with what little we have to survive, while at the same time seeing that it will never be the solution until we systematically change for the better and in the long run. We are mad that all the solutions and resources aren't working, but it was never meant to work without a true internal desire to see the educational system change, and get better because of true called individuals in the field that are there with intention instead of personal agendas.

The way that we can start off small is simple, number one, we can look at what we've done for centuries in education and get feedback from everyone possible on what it is that we know is NOT working. It would be simple, if you give anybody the chance to think and reflect on their own education, whether they are 19 years old or 59 years old, they will give you a whole list of various things that didn't help or work for them in education. Eventually as we look at all this feedback over time, we would begin to see that everyone is saying the same thing but in different ways. You're going to start finding that everyone is giving you the same information, and that same information is a major answer to the things we need to start taking a serious look at.

One of those things that everyone is saying in different ways currently, is this whole concept within education of keeping the community out of the loop, but at the same time claiming that there's no understanding of why they are not fully engaged. You will see that throughout this book I continue to say that. The communication within education right now is just like that old gum stuck to the bottom of your shoe on a hot day, that won't come off no matter how many times that you scrape and rub your foot on the ground. There have been minor changes and upgrades, but for the most part it's disgusting to see how little parents and families in general feel like they are only supplemental to the education of their students. Most of the communication is about academics and discipline, not about resources for families or things that can help students and families to be even more successful in the classroom. Once we start on communication, it's small, but it can be built upon.

Until we as society, as a country, as a nation, or as a field decide that WE want to get healthier in the realm of education, WE want students to survive in an ever changing working world, that WE want to see them successful long-term, nothing is going to change! Just like your heart or your body, when the doctor tells you to eat healthier, exercise, and you need to find a hobby to keep your mind going, if you as an individual don't do it, it's nobody's fault but your own!

Everything that we're seeing, the deficiencies, the corruption, the dysfunction, all of that is at the blame of EVERYONE directly and indirectly connected to the field of education. There is no one that can step back and say that they had no part to play in this! I myself have even had a part to play in it, because for so long and before my eyes were open to these types of things I could do, I was going along with what education was like when I was in school. So if we don't have that change, if we don't start opening our eyes to the things that we can start doing small to build on, when this system truly crashes and sinks, there's no one else we can blame but ourselves…the older generations. We can't sit back as students, teachers, or even retired individuals who just pay tax money to the schools, and say that it's not our fault. Because even when you put tax money into the system, you have a right to speak about the state of the district and where you expect your money to go. You have a right as an individual to join the school board or join committees within the district that will lead to those changes. You have a right to hold individuals accountable, whether it's the teacher, principal, or the superintendent. You have a right to hold these individuals accountable and pay attention to who is being given another contract or job, and who is not.

Therefore, if I or anyone else has not been doing that, when this system sinks or we look at the way it is now, we cannot sit back and say that it is not our fault. It is indeed our fault! As teachers we are supposed to be working with everyone in the community, and if we can't get everyone in the community to come and help us, then it is our job to work as professionals and determine ways we can bring those stakeholders in! Again, teachers are not superheroes in a sense that we can do everything that needs to be done to save people while continuing to mask our true identity. Teachers are also not experts, in that we are experts on all things education! Some of us have some really amazing skills and talents in specific areas of education, but we should not be expected to have the answers for everything in education. Lastly, teachers cannot do this without the other three parts! We need the students, parents, and administrators! Until we get all of those things in our minds, and we get all of those people engaged, we are going to continue to see what we see now! Education is a system and collective body! So just like when a person has been told to get their health together and there's nothing else that anyone can do for them, it's not up to the government, it's not up to other entities or individual people to help to bring this system back to where it should be. It takes ALL of us that are within education and connected to education, whether directly or indirectly, to WANT to see education healthy and sustained for the long-term. WE have to want it as much as everyone else....that's when we will see change!

CHAPTER 9

Future Teachers

If there's one thing that I wish I could travel around the world and speak to others about, it's those who are in college in teacher preparation programs. I know right now you're probably thinking "Well I don't know if I want to be a teacher, because I don't know if I can handle everything that's going on! I don't know if it'll change, so maybe I should reconsider what it is that I really want to do." The first thing I will say to you is STOP! Don't make a drastic decision based on a temporary situation. Right now I can admit, as someone that is in the field of education, yes it's crazy, it looks scary, and I don't know if all this that is going on right now would have caused me to leave my teacher preparation program. But you cannot base your career off of your emotions or the thoughts and suggestions of other people.

When I first went into education, as I mentioned before, I went into the field because I had a passion to change what it is that I experienced as a student many years ago. When I went into education I also knew that I wanted to be myself, I wanted to constantly be my authentic self to my students, because I knew that having a caring adult on campus is what would have made a huge difference in me as a student. So as you get ready to look forward to going into the classroom, the first thing that I suggest for you is to sit down and really ask yourself why it is that you're going into education. Why did you REALLY choose the field of education? Some people will ask you this question when you're in an interview, and the answers range anywhere from loving the moment a light switch goes on for a child to they always played pretend school as a child themselves. All of those answers sound nice and sweet, but that wasn't it for me! I truly believe that if educators were really honest with themselves, they would also say that those answers are not fully true for them either. Some people say those things, but it's much deeper than that!

Some people will honestly say that they got into education for the holidays off, the spring break, fall break, Christmas, summer, and so they could have the same schedule for their children. I don't have any hate towards anyone like that, you got into education for your reasons, and I got into education for my reasons. However, what I would ask them is whether that reason is going to keep you in education when you feel like quitting? That is also the next question I suggest you ask yourself! What is your reason for getting into education, and whatever that reason is, do you believe honestly that if all this stuff in education never changed that the reason you have is going to keep you in the field of education long term?

Now, some other advice that I would give to the new teachers coming into the field is number one, don't look on social media to get ideas on what you want to do in your classroom. What I find is that when you go on social media, and you look at other teachers and what they're doing in their classroom, you always feel like you need to do more or do better than what it is that you're already doing. All this will lead to your burnout, because you're trying to be someone else, and the one thing you always have to think about and keep in your mind is being your authentic self. Students will read you like the front page of a magazine cover as they are standing in the checkout line at the grocery store with their parents. I know that was a lot that I just said, but literally students read you! So here's a warning to you, if you haven't experienced someone reading you before, then it is going to be the most uncomfortable thing you experience the first time you step into a classroom. When they are reading you, they are looking at what you're wearing, what your face looks like, what your body language is, how you speak, what you say and don't say, who you're talking to compared to other students, what teachers do you hang with? They are going to look you up on social media, they will find your Instagram and tik tok, they are going to find everything there is to know about you, because they are reading you! Students do that not because they are trying to be stalkers or trying to be a personal investigator, but they are really trying to find out if you are really there for them? That's why you have to make sure that if you have social media or a presence in the community outside of school, that you remain your authentic self.

I can remember many times just being out in the grocery store (I tell my students all the time to be prepared for me to look bummy on weekends in public sometimes, they know it's my time to be authentically me), and they walk up to me and talk to me just like they do when I am on their school campus. There's no nervousness, there's no running behind their parents, there's no avoiding conversation, and their parents come talk to me as well. Why? Because I'm always my authentic self! Whether anyone has told you this before or not, if you're entering into the classroom…ALWAYS BE YOUR AUTHENTIC SELF! Do not try to force yourself to be cool. If you're a person that doesn't like video games, don't try to jump into a conversation with children about video games acting like you know about the video games…they will be able to tell that it's not really who you are! Doing that will actually cause you to be immediately pushed away from them, because they will question why you are being fake with them, and trying to be so cool! So always be your authentic self, and understand that when you are your authentic self, when you're in the community and live in the same area as your students, those students are going to walk up to you and introduce their parents to you. Not because you're doing such an amazing job in the classroom all the time, but because they feel your spirit and they feel your heart.

Another thing that I would suggest to individuals who are looking to join education is to turn off the negativity about education right now. It's kind of like when you were a child, and your parents tell you who you hang around is who you become. The same thing happens in education! If you listen to, read about, and watch on tv all the negative things that are going on in education, and then you go to a school and you only communicate with those who complain about education, you're eventually going to become someone that talks themselves out of the career that you really wanted for yourself. I myself feel like I was born and called to be a teacher. There are things that I see, that I experience, and that I do that other people have tried to shut down and be negative about, but it always brought something good for the students. So turn off the negativity surrounding education right now, and go find out for yourself what's going on! Don't always rely on the experiences or the words of others to determine your experiences when you become an education. Heads up, taking heed of this advice will cause a backlash. There will be some people who are upset because you don't sit in the teacher's lounge at lunch where all the gossip goes on. They will be upset because you don't go to happy hour, where everyone is trying to unload from last week, but you don't always have to explain why you don't do that. If your authentic self is to be positive and seek positives, even though sometimes you do want to get things off your chest, then you remember that and you turn off the negative! Always go to the school as an individual who is not just this motivational speaker, but always finding a way to remind yourself of the positive things that are happening right now!

A few of those positive things that I see in education right now are students who are a lot more serious about their education! They realized that when they were online, it was easier to get distracted, it was easy to just log in and not pay attention. I also see families that are closer together now! Parents have come to realize that whether online school was good or not for their child, they realized what information they didn't know about what was going on with the educational system, and have begun to see why it has been said by many teachers over the years that they need to be fully engaged instead of just involved. There ARE positive things going on within education, so again my advice to you is to turn off the negative things sometimes and find out for yourself!

Another thing that I would suggest for future teachers is to really start thinking about your students teaching early! Usually what happens when we get ready to do our student teaching is that the university will place us where they believe we fit. However, I have had unique experiences compared to others as an educator, and I'm about to share with you one of the biggest ones that showed me why some teachers are not always prepared or selected to teach initially.

I did my student teaching for an entire school year, I had to do two semesters, and it wasn't by choice! The first semester I did student teaching in a K-5th grade general education setting with another PE teacher, it was a school that was not Title 1, and there weren't many minority teachers. At this school, the personality of the other teacher and I were not complementary! That's another conversation or maybe even book for another day, but if your personalities don't mesh with another person, don't try to fake and become someone else. If you're in a school environment, and it seems like everyone is complaining about your personality, that's just your que to find an environment where your personality and who you are as a person is appreciated. Do not change yourself…I tried it for MANY years, and it does not work!

Anyways, I was at this school doing my student teaching that involved good interactions with the students, learning a lot, but this teacher didn't understand that I wasn't an extrovert. So the times that I was quiet and not interacting a lot, they took it as a sign of disrespect or that I didn't want to be there. Although that was the assumption, I was in fact being observant, because most of what we learn is when we are watching and listening more than talking! I even had students after my practicum was over that ended up reaching out to me via email about their experiences with some of the teachers. I responded to them, (now I see I should have just left it alone because I was not a certified teacher on that campus), and the other teacher didn't like it. After this, instead of having a conversation and training someone about this before they finish their program, they had decided that I was not ready to teach yet. In fact some of the comments I received were " I don't even know if this should be her final career choice, because she seems to be very quiet and standoffish. She should do one more semester of student teaching!"

So of course, as you can imagine, I had to do another semester of student teaching. When I went and did my next semester of student teaching, this was a school where there were more students with families who were considered low-income. I'm not saying that it was Title 1, (I've always felt called to Title 1 school environments) but this was a different school environment overall! At this school, when I initially met the other supervising teachers, they saw that I was quiet as well. One of the first things they may have thought was this would be a bad situation because I had "failed" the first semester of student teaching and had to do it all over again. They probably thought this would be a waste, because I didn't even speak that much to begin with, which most people assume means that a person is not called to teach. Let me be the first to say that not ALL teachers are extroverts!

However, they didn't do the same thing as the last teacher I worked with! Both of these individuals took the time to get to know me! They found out that I had a son, I was married at the time, I was kind of quiet by nature, that I loved various things, and I ended up passing that semester with flying colors! That's why my advice to you, as someone looking forward to a future within the field of education, YOU think about where YOU feel YOU would do best with student teaching! Sometimes where the university places you, you already know that it's not going to be a good fit! So start advocating for yourself, even if that means it puts you back a semester or delayed your graduation. Don't focus on that, it's temporary, because in the long run you want to be able to be in a setting where you can thrive as your authentic self while also building the skills that will make you an amazing teacher! If it takes longer, then that is just short term!

One more thing I would suggest about student teaching, is to see if it's possible for you to do your student teaching at an alternative school and general education during the same time frame. When I say alternative school, some people may immediately get nervous and say that they can't do it or weren't meant for it. The reason why I suggest this is because it wasn't until I was at the alternative school that I was able to build up the best classroom management and classroom culture. When I was at the alternative school, I learned that there are more important things than academics, policies, and others to get students to buy in and become fully engaged. It's about relationships, it's about connection, it's about love, it's about respect, it's about consistency and predictability. What I learned from the administrator was "If it's predictable, it is preventable!". This means that when you're in an alternative school setting, a lot of students thrive on consistency. They want to know when they come to school no matter what day, no matter what time or situation, they are going to get the same reaction every time. They want to know that if one student does something that is disrespectful, they are going to get the same consequence as another student that does the same thing. The only way that you really learn that the best is when you're in an alternative school setting, because if you mess up you will clearly see it! If you're inconsistent, if you're not authentic, if you're not caring, those students are definitely going to show you. Remember they are reading you! Again, when you start getting closer to student teaching, really start thinking about where you want to do the practicum, and where you feel you would be best as a future teacher! Start looking at the different schools in your area! You don't have to go to the schools, you can just look them up online and determine which ones you think may be a good fit. In fact, you can call the principal, have some questions already written about what you are looking for in your student teaching, and have a conversation about the school environment so that you are placed in the best place possible! You know best what seems like a good fit or not! It is important to build connections and insight before you are merely placed without prior knowledge...this was one of my biggest mistakes. I believe that if I did my student teaching at the second school the first time, I would not have had to do it over or even prove that I was competent and qualified.

So this chapter is my overall and broad advice to those who are in college, and looking forward to going into the field of education. Don't let yourself be discouraged right now! Don't run away from education, in fact I would encourage anyone who is looking into the field of education right now to consider that everything negative is the reason why you are being called to the field. All of the wrong is why YOU are needed, so that things can be made right, based on your experiences in education. YOU need to go and become the leader within the system to start creating change for the next generation!

Once you go and do great things, you can develop other teachers to do the same thing, and then it spreads. Remember, the ultimate sign of a leader is that they create other leaders without intimidation or jealousy! So if you're in your college dorm or sitting in a class, and you're wondering why you should continue going into education, stop first...don't run...just sit down and look at my advice! Really look at what legacy you would like to leave behind for the students coming behind you, that you don't want to have to experience the things that you did or maybe more of the positive things that you DID experience. However, don't run away from education, it's scary right now, it seems to be rocky, but it's one of the best fields that you can go into because it is something that allows you to plant the seeds that will grow and flourish for decades and centuries. In other words, remember one child that you plant the seed in is going to meet thousands of people for the rest of their lives, and sometimes it's a simple word or simple action that allows them, in front of those thousands of people, to be the life changer they felt called to be!

CHAPTER 10

Dismissal

As I conclude this book, I want to first make a statement that says I hope that the intentions of this book were clear and understood. It was never my intention to write a book about education, and have it be nothing but negative. Clearly I see more than the negative in education, because I have been invested in it for over ten years. However, the intentions of this book were to give a true, realistic, honest, and transparent look at not only what goes on inside some classrooms across the nation, but to give an absolute true and honest look at what teachers across this nation are going through.

Now, I may not have hit on everything that all teachers are going through, but a majority of what I've talked about is what I hear a lot of other teachers talking about. Sadly, these are not the things that have been heard on national tv. These are not the things that you will find on social media. On social media and on TV, what you see is a very negative narrative being pushed out and given to society and convinces people that all teachers are in the field for negative reasons.

This book hopefully helped you to understand that no matter what role you're in, there are good things happening within school and your individual child's classroom. There are negative things that are negative happening inside your child's classroom, and that is the reason why you have to be invested, you have to be engaged even if your child is just starting out!

When I started off this book I talked about a very traumatic situation that I remember from my 7th grade math teacher. Right now, whether we want to admit it or not, there are other students that are also sitting in 7th grade math enduring the same type of verbal and emotional abuse from math teachers. What's not understood is that when those types of things go on with teachers, even if it's not math, that is the reason why our children are not succeeding. If it was an easy solution like a different curriculum, a different program, or more curriculum and more resources, more summer school, more tutoring, then those things would be helping right now. If those things were such great solutions to the academic decline we see as adults, there would be no need to keep having discussions surrounding this. However, systematically we continue to see year after year after year that those things are not working. Students are still having struggles with certain areas of education. Most of the time if you take that child and get their feedback, as I have mentioned before, you will come to find out that it's more about relationship connections and caring adults on campus than it is about the curriculum.

I will always advocate for creativity in the classroom and for humanistic education. Meaning a teacher needs to realize that children are just younger versions of ourselves. They are not less intelligent. They are not less creative. They are not less capable. They are younger versions of ourselves, so when we step into the realm of education and we question why these solutions aren't working, we have to come to the realization that it's because of the perspectives of the adults in education and lack of student feedback on what we need to change for their success. When I say adults in education I'm not talking about the teachers. I'm not even always talking about administrators, I'm talking about those individuals that are in high up positions, even sometimes on a governmental level, who are making decisions about education and have never been in the classroom or maybe have stepped out of the classroom for more than ten to twenty years. You cannot make decisions and put laws in place, when you have not been in that environment over many years because there are things changing every single day.

Sometimes, what I find is when I speak as openly as I did in this book, there are a lot of people thinking that I am saying that I don't like education, that I'm just in education to complain. That is not true! What I've tried to do with this book, is to be a voice and to be an advocate of teachers across this nation. There are so many of us that are coming together in small ways because of what happened to us during the pandemic and quarantine, and we are saying

"How do we get this TRUE information out there more?" So this is my first step towards that!

I intend to write more books in the future about my life, maybe education, maybe my faith, maybe being a single parent! From this day first my intentions are to be a voice for the voiceless. I want to make sure that those who feel like they are not being heard, those that feel like they don't have an opportunity to speak, or when they speak it's too loud for anyone that tries to listen, to know that someone is out there trying to support and stand with them.

To those of you that are future teachers, just like in the last chapter, please turn off the negative media regarding education and find out for yourself what's going on in education. When I first started out in education, before I received my certification, I actually worked at an after school program in an elementary school. Not only did it help me to see the ins and outs of being in an elementary school, but it also showed me that I might not want to be on the elementary school level for the rest of my career. I also went and was a substitute teacher for some time, after I was done with my practicum of course. Student teaching allowed me to see what level of education I wanted to be on initially (elementary, middle school, high school), did I want to do the traditional schedule or block schedule, would I ever consider doing after school programs and school sports, what are the different ways to connect with students on different school levels, the type of administration I would prefer to be around, it was a lot of information that I gleaned from doing substitute teaching. So for my future teachers, please take from my advice, and go out there and prepare yourselves! Go find out where you feel you would do best, where you would fit best, and don't allow yourself or anyone else to continue to shift you around and push you around like what has happened to me over these years.

To my current teachers in the field right now, I first want to say that I love you guys! I support you, I see you, I hear you, and I am standing with you. We may not all agree on the same thing, there may be certain topics or issues that we don't see eye to eye on, but at the end of the day we are all educators and we haven't left. As much as it hurts every day to go experience what we experience in these classrooms with these students and sometimes even families…we're still here! So I'm proud of you for sticking to it, I'm proud of you for getting up every day and remembering your why! Why do you truly and deeply stay in education? What keeps you in the field after all these years? And don't ever forget that! Don't ever allow yourself to get into so much toxicity that you forget why you're there. Even if you don't necessarily have a reason, you just feel like you were called to the field of education, think about your own educational experiences when you were in grade school. Think about the teachers that you had really good connections with, think about the teachers that you didn't have really good connections with, and let that lead you, push you, and motivate you to continue to do what you do every day in the classroom. I know that just like me, you see teachers that you feel shouldn't be in the classroom. I know that just like me, you see administration that shouldn't be in schools, but the only way that we're going to make this thing better is if we see those things, but we take it upon ourselves to be intentional about making things by putting it in action! Doing the things that we speak about and think about.

I also want to give another piece of advice to my teachers who are in the classroom right now...STOP SELF-SACRIFICING! So much of your time is spent helping and thinking about helping somebody else, whether it's somebody else's children or another adult...stop doing that!

I'm not saying don't ever have a kind or giving heart or be there for others, but stop selfsacrificing yourself! Stop trying to push down the fact that you ARE tired, that you DO need rest, that you DO need a break, and keep pushing through to do things for other people. As long as we continue to do this as teachers within the field, there will be no need for changes to be made regarding PTO, conferences, budgets, etc. What you're doing (myself included) my doing this is showing that the little you are always given will be just enough! So if you know you can't REALLY afford to buy school supplies or things for your students...STOP DOING IT! If you do not want to do anymore after school activities and clubs...STOP DOING IT! If you need to take a day off just for a mental day or a day of quietness while your own children are at school...DO IT! A lot of us are doing things out of habit, but not realizing that we are teaching others in the field how to treat us. Continuing to self-sacrifice in burning you out, and you're also sacrificing your time with your family and children.

I know it's hard, because it's something that I have to work on every day! I remember years where I was doing so much for other children that I would come home to hear my son say that he felt neglected....that's when things shifted! So now put yourself first! If you're a believer like me, you know the order that God expects us to hold in our life regarding taking care of things in life! Recognize that even when you decide to put your family first, you're not forgetting about yourself or neglecting yourself! As you prepare your lesson plans, work on those during the week during your preps while you're eating if you have to, there's nothing wrong with eating in your classroom and not in the lounge hearing all the latest gossip...trust me, you'll enjoy not "being in the loop" sometimes! In the evenings and on the weekend, don't take your laptop home! Start doing like myself, if it doesn't get done at work, it'll stay at work until you pick it up the next day! You might go through a little stress, might have anxiety because you're so used to bringing work home, but when you finally see that you can leave work at work and go home to relax, you will fully understand why I told you to start doing all of this. PLEASE SELFSACRIFICING...it's not worth it. In fact you're probably killing yourself and lessening your health because of it!

To the administrators that read this book, maybe you've read this book and you feel like I shouldn't be in the field of education, or maybe you read this book and you wish that some of the teachers around you had told you this information that I shared. Or maybe you read this book and you want to talk to me! I'm open to talk, but here's the thing, I will always be completely honest! A lot of administrators don't understand, your administrative certification didn't change anything about you. I talked about this in a previous chapter, but all that it did was say that you're qualified to do that job! It didn't change your heart, it didn't change your overall knowledge, it didn't change your effort to build a quality culture and climate on the school campus. So please do all of us teachers a favor, and stop reminding us that you're "above us"! We know that you get paid more, we know that you're in a higher position than us, but we don't need to be reminded of that every day. Instead of doing that, instead of always carrying a title, carry a mantle of true togetherness on your campus! Help educators to see that if they aspire to be an administrator like yourself, they can be an administrator, and you will be there to help them develop into an amazing leader. Help staff to come to campus every day and feel supported! Sometimes being supportive is just getting to know a person. There are a lot of introverted teachers, and sometimes you probably don't notice that they are introverts, because a lot of people assume that to be a teacher means you must be an extrovert...that's not the case. I'm in fact an introvert, I have more introverted tendencies than the average teacher. So most times, the administration takes my quietness or the fact that I observe more than I speak as disrespect.

Get to know your people! A lot of you say that everyone within the school building is part of a "school family". However, I can almost guarantee that there is someone on your campus that does not feel like they are a part of that family. They don't feel that family culture. They don't feel connected with everyone like that! In fact, they may even feel like the step-child that is being isolated because they don't carry the same last name as everyone else in the family. So please get to know your people! Spend more time throughout the year, instead of just at the beginning of the year, getting to know who your teachers REALLY are! And if you have a teacher on your campus that is standoffish or not really taking the time to allow you to get to know them, don't tell them that they have walls up and are hard to approach. Give them grace and mercy, and recognize that they may have gone through a lot of stuff in their life that has trained them not to trust everyone. It's your time to give them a reason to trust you and others, rather than judging them and making them out to be an issue on campus. Get to know your people!

Another thing that I would say to the administration…please stop using cliché' words and terms. There are enough years behind a lot of us teachers to know if you really mean what you say. If you say you support your staff…show it! If you say you love your staff…show it! I have not been in an official administrative role yet within the individual school campus setting, but I have always been given administrative responsibilities. One of the things I like to tell those who I have worked with during these administrative responsibilities, sometimes even my students and families, is I will never ask you to do anything I'm not willing to do and I'm not going to say anything that I don't genuinely feel. That's my advice to you! If you would not do something that you're asking your teachers and your staff to do, then don't even ask them to do it either. If you really don't feel it in your heart when you say something, then don't say it to your teachers and staff. Just like students read teachers, teachers read administration and we can definitely tell when you're being insecure and fake.

To families, you guys know that you have my heart! My doctorate research was all about parental engagement and family engagement. I have done so many events over the years both in and out of the school setting to bring people together. Most recently I've done a book drive, and before that it was a backpack and school supply drive. I've always felt like the major missing link is for teachers to show a true desire to be connected and engaged with families. I don't know how much more I can emphasize the importance of needing you guys. I don't care if you're a single parent, I don't care if you were previously incarcerated, I don't care if you're a high school or college dropout, I don't care if you're so educated that I can't understand the words that you say! I'm not here to judge, I'm here to bring people together, but the thing about is that you have to do the same thing!

If you had bad experiences when you were in grade school please don't judge us and project that on us! Please don't come to the school with your child and assume that we are going to be the same way. A lot of us have had bad experiences, especially those of us born in the 80s and raised in the 90s, we've probably had the same type of educational experiences. Guess what though? Some of us, like myself, are trying to change that for the next generation, and is part of the reason that we even chose to go into the field of education. You have to give us a chance! Don't just drop your children off, throughout the school year, and assume that everything is good or ok. As I talked about before, go and examine those teachers! You have a right to come into our classrooms, and if there's ever a teacher that doesn't want you to come into their classroom or makes you feel uncomfortable about doing so, then that's something that you need to bring to the administration's attention. Know the chain of command! If you or your child has an issue go to the teacher, if that doesn't work out you go to the principal, if that doesn't work out you go to the district office. Understand that when you go to the district office, those individuals are not above you. You're not inferior to them! They are community members that took it upon themselves to take on those roles and positions to try and create positivity in the district. So if you take your concerns to them, and you don't feel like they are fulfilling that role, it is your right to step up and talk or continue talking and going up the chain of command! Don't just let individuals in these schools do whatever they want to do or think is best to do without your input for your child! You know what's best, and those of us that appreciate you will make it our mission to include you in everything regarding your child, even outside of academics and discipline…you're our family too! We need you! Most of the issues and concerns that we see right now in education stem from the fact that there are not enough parents that are stepping up and talking!

When it comes to your children, I would advise you to listen to them! Yes sometimes teenagers will lie to get their way, but for the most part take your child's words as truth! There are a lot of children right now that are enduring abuse and different things in the classroom. When I tell them to tell their parents, they say that they don't want to because they know that you won't believe them. We have to stop that! There are a lot of children who need you to be a parent, they need you to listen, they need you to hear them and support them. Sometimes support for these young people is just your simply listening to them when they are speaking truthfully about what is going on in the classroom. Instead of turning away, reflect on the way that your teachers were when you were in grade school, not much has changed, and take the time to investigate the situation. When young people have parents that do that, they feel like they really are protected no matter what!

I love your children like they are my own child, but there is only so much I can do without your support! Just like with me being a single mother right now, I can't do all there is to be done to raise a male child, and I can't do all there is to be done with raising up a whole generation of successful youth in the younger generation without you! Please make sure that you take your children's words as truth, and that you truly find out the best ways you can support them! Sometimes that may even mean letting them control the radio in the car, or going to a place you don't want to go to but they do. These children right now need a lot more emotional connection, and they cannot get it all from us at the school!

Students....I didn't forget you! Keep on doing what you're doing, keep working hard and don't talk back to the teachers. If they are disrespectful to you, go get your parents involved, you shouldn't have to do that on your own or take it into your own hands. Trust me, the stories I have shared with you about when I took things into my own hands weren't good, and I don't want you to repeat the mistakes I made doing that. Also, understand that your education is something that can never be stolen. Once you get your education there is no way that anyone could ever take it from you. It's in your brain cells, it's in your soul, it's in your thoughts, it's in your words…it can't be taken away. So don't go into school thinking that it's pointless, yes you're not going to use everything that you learn in the classroom, but a lot of it you are. Why would you allow anyone to steal something from you, to take something from you that once you get it no one can ever remove it from you?

Every day you go to class I want you to be reminded of the fact that there is a purpose that you are here on this earth. You are on this earth for something only you can do, even if it's to teach, there is a specific way that you will teach that no one else can do. If it's to design or if it's to be a police officer, if it's to be a nurse, there is something that only you can do and it's important that you understand that now as a young person. When you journey through this life, a lot of people are going to try and tell you what to be. Trust me, if you listen to those people and you try to do what everyone else tells you to do, you're going to be my age when you finally come to realize what your purpose is on this earth. You're also going to be mad because you wasted so much time trying to be a copy of someone else! Don't be a repeat, don't be a copy, don't be a robot...be yourself all the time! If you don't know you are as yourself, take some time to sit with instrumental music, and make a list of the things that you DO enjoy, those things that you DON'T enjoy, those things that you like for people to do to show appreciation, and those things that you DON'T like for people to do that makes you insecure.

Don't EVER question your worth! Don't EVER question your beauty! Don't EVER question if you're good enough, you are good enough and you're perfectly fine being who you are right now! I say that as someone who has struggled with insecurities about my worth and what my purpose is on this earth for most of my life. Don't repeat me! Don't do the things that I used to do when I was a young person, go and be better than me! Go further than me...do something with your life that is going to empower me!

I love you all SO MUCH, and I'm glad that I have had many conversations over the years with all of you to help me to become a better person and a better teacher! It is because of all of you (students, teachers, administrators, families, etc.) that I started and have completed writing this book!

Thank you for encouraging me to write this book, whether you did it by being a supporter or disrespectful or hateful. I hope I did this justice, I hope you all actually read the entire book, and I hope it's something that you continue to go back to when you have those rough days and storms while navigating through life, school, or being a parent. Those types of days and seasons are going to come! Like I said, don't ever give up! Don't ever question yourself, because you're royalty and you're a king or queen…so act like it!

Made in the USA
Columbia, SC
08 July 2022